52

LEADERSHIP
TIPS

That Will Change
How You Lead Others

GREG L. THOMAS

Printed in the United States of America

Published by WingSpan Press, Livermore, CA

www.wingspanpress.com

The WingSpan name, logo and colophon are the trademarks of WingSpan Publishing.

EAN 978-1-59594-089-6

ISBN 1-59594-089-8

First Edition 2006

Library of Congress Control Number 2006932639

DEDICATION & ACKNOWLEDGEMENT

I would like to dedicate this book to all those who have given me their time and love throughout my life. No man is an island, and what I am today is the product of the wisdom, correction, challenges and joy they have brought into my life.

• To my wife BJ, whose enduring love and personal example of caring are a continual inspiration to me. I love you...

• To my three jewels, no man could have ever received more wonderful daughters than Kelly, Karyn and Kathleen. The three of you have taught me more than you will ever know (or that I am willing to admit). A special thanks to my son-in-law Joe Mango for his editing skills to make this book better.

• To my parents, I can never thank you enough for the love, values and work ethic you taught me as a child. Your example taught me that education, hard work and drive would lead to a life of accomplishment. I can never repay you for your caring sacrifice and diligence to teach me right from wrong as a boy and teenager.

• To Ambassador College, my deepest gratitude for taking a gawky and inexperienced twenty-two year old kid from Cleveland and helping him to discover himself, his Creator, and his great potential. Your values still live on in my heart.

• To Bellevue University, it was your Masters program in Leadership that sparked a fire within me that still burns brightly! Without your excellent program, my love for leadership and this book would never have happened.

• To Howard Baker, thank you for being a mentor and for your personal example of servant leadership.

TABLE OF CONTENTS

Chapter 4 – Develop Your Leadership Skills

Chapter 5 – A Few Modern Leadership Theories

INTRODUCTION

I entered the business world in the early 1970's and have had many roles. I have been an electrician, construction estimator, marketing manager, national & regional sales manager, author, editor and founder of a small nonprofit organization.

By age thirty-two, I was the National Sales Manager for a *Fortune 100 Corporation* that sold electrical transformers throughout North America. I was given the responsibility to manage over 100 salesmen at 30 representative agencies, and 100 million dollars in sales (in today's dollars). What I began to learn early in my career was how dysfunctional virtually all organizations are. Almost all are based on a diseased premise that limits their growth and stunts the potential of their people. This false premise is the belief that effective management should be *autocratic* to be effective. To support this approach, bloated hierarchies must be constructed, and people must be controlled at every level. This nurtures a "command and control" executive philosophy that becomes obsessed with making hundreds of rules and policies to keep people in their place.

Those at the top of the pyramid believe themselves to be *superior* and the *most* talented. They build an organization that rewards the uncreative but compliant while punishing the talented who ask too many embarrassing questions. This culture usually creates three general types of people in this working environment:

1. The ambitious and compliant individuals who want to make it to the top at any cost or personal sacrifice.

They take great pleasure in their titles and telling others they work at "headquarters." They get to spend their careers dealing with meaningless and *unproductive* meetings, conference calls, contradictory strategy sessions, information overload, political jockeying and managing the next large group of alienated personnel.

2. The vast majority who slowly become disillusioned and just go through the motions everyday. They come to a point where they only work for a paycheck. These individuals become very skilled at *pretending* they are productive or care. They cleverly make mere activity look like they are really accomplishing something. Their major goal on the job is to get out of the organization at 5 o'clock, or preferably forever by finding a better job. Imagine the productivity lost and the talent undiscovered!

3. Those employees who get sick of dealing with "hindquarters" take their talents where they are appreciated. Many of these individuals become the *entrepreneurs* and innovators of new businesses. There is a reason that the overwhelming number of new jobs created in the United States are by small business owners! Most of these small businesses are started by men and woman who got sick of working with the mental midgets who control corporate life.

Within a few months of hiring, virtually every new employee gravitates toward one of these three categories.

The good news is that this condition fosters many entrepreneurs and successful new businesses. The bad news is that as these new businesses grow, many of them eventually become dysfunctional by default. The aging founders, or the next generation, become what they despised the most... autocratic, bloated and ineffective. Without real leadership every organizational culture evolves to become toxic. As regarding organizations, Steven Covey states in his book, *The 8th Habit*, "To some degree, they're all a mess."

But there is an alternative! It is known by many names, including servant leadership, stewardship, authentic leadership or principle-centered leadership. It has been around for thousands of years but was reintroduced in the modern age by a man named Robert Greenleaf. It is a totally different leadership approach which also has organization, structure, strategy, rules, policies and professionalism. But what makes it different is the ability to energize all employees to become innovative problem solvers. They become far more productive and take *ownership* in their work. They tap into their suppressed potential and begin to lead themselves and others. In turn, leadership begins to permeate every level of the organization. Most of all, people enjoy their careers, and they bring "heart" into the workplace. Is this really possible? Yes, but at its *core* is the desire to serve others first, and this attitude prepares you to really lead others effectively.

However, none of this can even begin to happen unless you take a 180 degree turn from everything you have always assumed and have been taught in the corporate zoo! Autocratic management is a social disease that sickens everyone who comes in contact with it. It destroys human creativity and innovation.

Thankfully we have a number of highly successful companies that have adopted a servant leadership approach, and it has made them unique. These include organizations like Southwest Airlines®, Synovis Financial®, Aflac®, The Container Store®, Vanguard Investment Group®, Men's Warehouse®, TDIndustries®, and many others. Today over 20% of *Fortune Magazine's "Top 100 Best Companies to Work For"* subscribe to servant-leadership principles!

These are not organizations that exist in pampered high margin markets with no competitors. They face competitive pressures that would make most CEO's cry themselves to sleep at night. In spite of this, they thrive because they have found the key that will make them great and successful in the long-term.

These companies are not on a pedestal; they are not perfect, and they often face serious challenges like all other organizations. What makes them different?

They discovered that their greatest asset and most untapped natural resource is their people. They know that this is the *Knowledge Worker Age*, and no longer do they manage or control people like they do things.

This is the reason weLEAD Incorporated was started in 2001 and why this book was written. This book offers you 52 leadership tips that will change how you view the purpose of management and how you lead others. Each tip is intended to be read and meditated upon for a week. The 52 tips in this book will help you *reinvent* yourself over the period of a year. These tips were originally published in *weLEAD Online Magazine* over a 4 year period. Each one has been edited and updated for this book. There is no revolutionary information in this book. What I have been able to do is collect the most effective leadership skills and concepts available today and present them in a clear and concise manner. In the past few years, I have read and reviewed for weLEAD over 100 leadership books available on the market today. These 52 leadership tips are my collection of the best management information now available, and they produce positive results.

There are no quick fixes in life. After reading each weekly tip, I encourage you to reflect on the thoughts and ideas presented. Spend the week practicing the skills presented and develop the habit of servant-leadership. Most of the tips offer *practical* steps or advice to guide you toward developing the qualities of a servant leader.

A few years ago I finished providing a keynote address on servant-leadership to a group of engineers. When I was done, a man in his 40's approached me with his hand extended to shake my hand. He said, "If I had only known about these principles, it would not only have changed how I manage others but how I live my life! I would have been a better husband, father and son. I would have handled problems differently and not with an overbearing approach." I responded that once you realize that being a "servant" is the core to genuine leadership, it changes how you view life and other people. The lesson here is that these principles are *not* only for business relationships.

Allow this book and leadership philosophy to change you. Then you can become an example and a mentor to others. If you work for an autocratic boss or organization, you can still demonstrate these traits in your small area of influence. Model these principles in your department and with those whom you have daily contact with. Lead those who work under you as a genuine servant leader. A small seed can grow into a large tree. Finally, *lead up* to your boss whether it seems to be appreciated or not. It may be an uphill battle. Sadly most autocratic cultures are toxic, but make the commitment to "stand in the gap" and make a real difference.

Revolutions occur one heart at a time...

Greg L. Thomas

Chapter 1

HAVING A RIGHT LEADERSHIP PHILOSOPHY

It is essential to have the right approach and perspective about leadership. How well you lead will be determined by your personal mission, values, and goals. When these are balanced and in harmony, they provide the right motive to lead.

UNDERSTANDING LEADERSHIP IN THE 21ST CENTURY

As we enter the 21st century there is a growing awareness of the importance and need for *effective* leadership. The critical need to develop real leaders is so prevalent that many universities now offer graduate programs in leadership studies. It appears that a serious examination of leadership qualities has come of age and is finally receiving its proper recognition. There are literally dozens of various definitions of leadership. We will simply provide one that we feel effectively defines organizational leadership in virtually all situations.

"Leadership is the ability to articulate a vision, to embrace the values of that vision, and nurture an environment where everyone is motivated to reach the organization's goals and their own personal needs."

Effective modern leadership is a skill comprised of many different traits or qualities. Some of these qualities include vision, a mission, values, commitment, motivation, and consensus building. The *lack* of any of these important traits or qualities may greatly reduce the effectiveness of a leader. Here is a very brief definition of these qualities.

Vision: The meaningful articulation of the mission of the organization in such an appealing and intuitive picture that it vividly conveys what it can be like in a *better* future. Vision instills a common purpose, self-esteem and a sense of membership within the organization. Traditionally, vision has come exclusively from the top management or the founder. However, many leaders are now also beginning to see the value of creating a corporate vision by *including* the members who are closer to the work environment and the customer.

Mission or Mission Statement: This typically describes the purpose of the organization and outlines the types of activities to be performed for constituents and customers. It should also mention what unique value or services the organization offers as a byproduct of its efforts. Mission statements typically contain at least three components. First, a statement of the overall *purpose* or mission of the company is declared. Secondly, a statement that indicates the *values* that employees are expected to maintain in the daily decision-making process. Third, a declaration of the *major goals* that management believes is essential to attain the mission. These goals should be consistent with the philosophical values that employees are expected to maintain.

Values: These are the guiding principles that state how the employees, beginning with management, intend to conduct their business and their behavior. These values will determine what kind of an organization develops and they become the foundation of the organizations culture.

Commitment: This is an employee's emotional investment to extend great effort toward the realization of a decision, outcome or goal. Successful leaders need to set a *personal example* of commitment to inspire others to achieve the organizations established goals, and the ultimate mission.

Motivation: This is the ability to provide an incentive or reason to compel others into action or a commitment. Since all individuals are different, successful leaders know that diverse people respond to different motivators. A wise leader also knows that money is not the strongest long-term motivator and cultivating an environment of *fear* is the least effective long-term motivator.

Consensus Building: This is the ability of a leader to build an agreement among differing individuals within a group. A consensus usually occurs when various members of a group agree that a particular alternative is acceptable though it may not have been the *first* choice of each member. Consensus building can create a greater degree of commitment among group members than a decision make by a simple majority. However, consensus building requires additional discussion time and sometimes may not be possible. Eventually the leader may need to take the initiative, and affirm that the group decision has been made in order to begin implementation.

The valuable purpose of leadership in our modern age is to provide vision, direction and motivation for a team of individuals to accomplish a task or mission that otherwise could not be accomplished by a single individual. Other members of the group, team or organization are called "followers." Followers are those who subscribe to the vision and guidance of the leader.

The study of *followership* is also of growing interest. However, don't be confused by the term followers or followership. This term should never be used in a derogatory or negative setting. Followers may also exhibit leadership qualities in order to achieve their own tasks and individual roles. Followership is an important necessity and responsibility! Many of today's most effective leaders first learned to be good followers before they acquired the skills, opportunity and experience to lead others. In other words, learning and appreciating the skills of followership are often the reason an individual has gained the experience and necessary knowledge to become a leader.

Wise leaders are beginning to understand that it is their responsibility to develop followership by encouraging wider participation in corporate goal setting and objectives. Modern leaders are viewing followers as *partners* in the enterprise who should be encouraged to pursue innovation and given the empowerment to do their jobs well. There is very little evidence that the so-called "naturally born" leader really exists. Ongoing leadership studies are showing that the concept of a "natural born" leader has little merit. One reason for this error may be that people often mistake charisma for leadership. It is true that some leaders possess a great amount of personal charm or charisma. However, most leaders do not. In reality, leaders are not born, they are shaped by many factors. Some factors that often forge effective leadership traits are education, preparation, experience and opportunity.

Why is leadership important to you? It is important because the development of positive leadership skills can have a beneficial and powerful impact in virtually every area of your life! Acquiring leadership skills can have a constructive influence within your workplace environment, within your community and in your personal relationships with others. I encourage you to take advantage of the vast amount of knowledge now available within the growing study of leadership.

Consider that it was Harry S. Truman, who once said, "Men make history and not the other way around. In periods where there is no leadership, society stands still. Progress occurs when courageous, skillful leaders seize the opportunity to change things for the better."

WHAT LEADERSHIP IS NOT

During the last 50 years we have experienced an explosion of books and consultants focused on promoting management and leadership. Yet the fact remains that much confusion exists today, even about the very *definition* of the word leadership! In our modern society we have yet to distinguish between two opposing roles. The positive role of those individuals who *beneficially* change our lives and organizations with remarkable achievement, and the highly destructive who simply claw their way to the top of their heap! We have a terrible cultural tendency of calling them *both* leaders!

Take just one look at the daily news and you will easily see what I mean. For example, when speaking of an international meeting *including* political tyrants and dictators, the media will typically proclaim something like "today world leaders gathered." In a similar way, you may hear how a CEO or business executive has been convicted of a criminal act, yet they are typically referred to as a "business leader!" Sadly, we still call individuals *leaders* simply because they gained control of an organization. We use this term loosely no matter how they arrived at that position or how ineptly they have managed. Think about this fact; in what other setting could we be allowed to put individuals like Thomas Jefferson, Abraham Lincoln, Winston Churchill, Martin Luther King, Adolph Hitler, Joseph Stalin and Sadam Hussein in the same classification!

In our western culture we have made a few feeble attempts to distinguish between these vastly different types of achievers. Some authors and management consultants have coined beneficial phrases like *servant leadership, stewardship or principle-centered leadership* to draw a distinction, but with little effect. Yet, we continue to degrade the real position and achievement of those who guided others to attain incredible progress, while artificially granting status to those whose lives were dedicated to manipulation and control over others. We do this by calling them both...leaders. As a society, we obviously have not gotten to the point where we are ready to dogmatically articulate the difference. I am committed to drawing this clear distinction and emphasizing the difference between those who merely seek to "command and control" others, in contrast to those who truly lead others with an attitude of service demonstrated by positive core values.

I am a strong advocate of what is now called the servant leadership or stewardship philosophy. A real modern leader is a servant first! Secondly, the servant leader aspires to lead in order to help produce positive change. The leader's main goal is to help the followers *grow* as individuals. This allows them the freedom to meet their needs and goals as they become more autonomous, wiser and productive. In turn, they also become servant leaders since they will model those who have earned credibility and their respect. I believe you can become an "army of one" in your organization and begin to influence many co-workers by being a servant leader. Others will notice the difference. Maybe you can't single-handedly change the culture or environment of your organization, but you can change *yourself* as a great beginning. Those co-workers who work for you and with you will notice the difference!

Our ultimate goal should be to articulate a new set of terms to distinguish between the positive role of a leader whose service beneficially changes our world, in contrast to the *anti-leaders* who simply exist to serve themselves and their ego at the expense of others. This will not be an easy task, but it must begin somewhere. It is going to begin right here and now.

For further reading on this topic I encourage you to read *Beyond Counterfeit Leadership* by Ken Shelton. Ken is the Executive Editor of Executive Excellence Publishing and he often speaks boldly on this important issue.

Consider that it was Horace Mann, who once said, "Be ashamed to die until you have won some victory for humanity."

WHAT IS YOUR PERSONAL MISSION STATEMENT?
PART 1

Business today is complex and vulnerable. Any organization that wishes to survive must have a clear "mission statement" and an unquenchable drive to achieve it. A mission statement for a business describes the *purpose* of the organization and outlines the types of activities to be performed for constituents and customers. It should also mention what unique value or services the organization offers as a byproduct of its work.

However, *life* is also very complex in today's world and to maximize our individual potential and opportunities we should also have a "personal mission statement." What is yours? Your personal mission statement is your *own* particular "constitution" that reflects your unique purpose and values! It will help to *focus* your energies and resources. It will also provide a sense of orientation and unify the fragments of your life.

Here are some sound reasons why you should invest the time to create your own *personal* mission statement. Ponder these good reasons to establish one in your life.

- It defines what I stand for. This is often referred to as a belief system. This includes deeply held principles, including your degree of spirituality. For most, this is the foundation upon which their lives are built.

- It defines what I value. Your values should be your moral compass. This is a great aid, particularly during difficult times in life when your ethics or standards are under assault.

- It clarifies my essential mission in life. If you can't articulate your essential mission, the process of creating your personal mission statement will prod you to ponder this essential question.

- It outlines my responsibilities. Many leaders ultimately fail because they either forget their personal responsibilities to others or falsely believe they are "above" normal expectations.

Things to remember in the creation of your mission statement...

It is yours only! Personalize it for you. This is your special assignment and creation. Take the time to ask yourself some heartfelt questions and search for clear responses. Your personal mission statement is supposed to be different than everyone else's. You are unique!

Make it as short or as long as you want. There is not a "hard and fast" rule, but if you want to frame it to hang on a wall, it will need to be succinct to be readable in limited space.

Work on it until it inspires you. The idea is for this document to motivate you when it is referred to in the future. It should reflect not just the way you are today, but what you hope to become in a better tomorrow! Remember that leaders are visionaries who seek to improve the world or business they live in.

Now what do we do with it?

- It should be written and made public at home! Take pride and ownership in this document. If you are really bold you may want to display it in the workplace on your desk or wall at the office!

- It should be reviewed at least once per week. A good suggestion is to do this as part of a weekly meditation. If you are a spiritual person, perhaps the time you set aside for religious observances would be ideal.

- It should provoke humble self-analysis. Your personal mission statement will provide a "benchmark" to evaluate your present level of personal growth and development. This should not only include reflection on what still needs to be done, but on the achievements accomplished to this point in time.

- It should be allowed to be re-written as we grow and change. In time we all change and hopefully mature as we grow through life's experiences. Expect to make adjustments to your goals and desires, as they will shift with age.

In the next tip, we will discuss how to write the basic parts of your own personal mission statement!

Consider that it Robert Browning who wrote, "Ah, but a man's reach should exceed his grasp, or what's a heaven for?"

WHAT IS YOUR PERSONAL MISSION STATEMENT? PART 2

In this tip we continue to discuss why and how you should create your own personal mission statement. When sitting down to write your own mission statement, remember that it should be composed of at least four basic parts. If your mission statement is too short, it will be ambiguous and have very little real meaning (some organizations suffer from the same problem). On the other hand, if it is too long, it will lose its motivational impact and read like a journal. Four to five paragraphs is a good readable length.

Here are the *four* basic parts that I recommend be included as part of your document.

> *Part 1*—Stating and confirming your belief system and values.
>
> *Part 2*—Personal family goals...Achieving personal goals as a loving parent, supportive spouse, and nurturing your children.
>
> *Part 3*—Personal career goals...Attaining job satisfaction, confirming the purpose of your career, and developing greater skills.
>
> *Part 4*—Personal life goals...pursuing education, enhancing spiritual development, extending talents, maintaining health, serving others, developing a proper attitude, cultivating loving relationships, practicing philanthropy, etc.

Here are some more details on what it should include:

Beliefs and values. What is your moral code? What values give guidance to your daily life? Whether it is the "golden rule", religious scriptures or another source, this is where you should begin! In this opening paragraph of your mission statement, strongly state your deeply held ethical principles and moral code. If you haven't thought intensely about this before, it could be the most revealing part of your mission statement.

Personal family goals. This includes your relationship with your parent(s), spouse, and children. If you want a happy and balanced family life, you also need to have these essential goals. Of course, input from all family members will make these goals more attainable and fun to achieve! How do you want to "coach" each member to become all they can possibly be?

Personal career goals. Why do you work? Is it to find personal fulfillment or simply to generate income for other interests in life? Do you want to change your career path? If so, how do you plan on making this change? Are there career skills you want to enhance or acquire? At the end of your career, what do you want others to say about your contribution in the workplace?

Personal life goals. This part includes some of the most satisfying aspects of human life, and sadly most people put these off until retirement or forever! How do you plan on maintaining a healthy body and mind? Do you need more education to fulfill a lifelong personal goal?

Do you desire to "give back" to others for the blessings you have been granted? What would you do for the rest of your life if money were not a limitation? Now it is time to sit down in a quiet environment, listen to your heart and write.

Remember that this is *your* personal mission statement. Don't rush the process, let your creativity express what is in your heart. Allow this document to be a vital *extension* of you! Take pride and ownership in what you write. If you get a feeling of mental gridlock, step away for a few hours and come back to it later. Work on it until the document reflects what you truly feel and believe. Allow your personal mission statement to inspire you.

Good Luck and if you get stuck or need any help feel free to email me at gthomas@leadingtoday.org.

Consider that it was Mark Twain who said, "Let us endeavor so to live that when we come to die even the undertaker will be sorry."

LEADERSHIP GOALS?

The establishment and completion of *goals* is essential to sound leadership. Goals are important for a number of reasons. They provide direction toward the completion of responsibilities and duties. They encourage us to find more efficient ways to work.

They provide a benchmark for us to later evaluate our performance and make needed changes or adjustments. Finally, the *right goals* can be both challenging and motivating, which in turn can improve our personal performance. We may also need to help establish goals for others who work with us. If so, we must realize that goals should be used to clarify the expectations of others and should never be established to control or punish other people. Here are a *few* important things to remember when establishing goals for yourself or others.

Establish relevant goals that are related to your primary activities and needs. Remember that rival goals *compete* for your time, energy and attention. Important activities that have no established goals will most likely be neglected. Take the time to determine which activities and needs are primary and which are secondary. We are only capable of *focusing* on a limited number of activities at any one time.

Establish goals that are specific and clear. Rather than "setting a goal" that only achieves a simple activity, establish *measurable* objectives and a timeline for achievement. Include specific activities that can be performed to achieve the overall goal. Often a *series* of minor steps or "mini goals" can be taken to achieve the established primary goal. Remember that a large task may seem virtually impossible to accomplish until we break it down into smaller achievable steps.

Establish goals that are challenging yet realistic. For the goal to be motivating, it is important to strike a balance in its level of difficulty. The goal must be a challenge that will *stretch* our present capabilities. If it is too easy or requires very little effort it becomes meaningless. However, it should not be so difficult that it appears unrealistic and becomes demoralizing.

Collaborate with others in setting goals. If your task is to help establish goals for others, you *must* get their input for it to be effective and meaningful to them. Their level of commitment will be dramatically increased when *your* goals for them, and their *own* personal goals can be mutually blended. Even when establishing your own goals, input from others may provide you with a different perspective or priority.

Write the goals down! Numerous studies have shown there is a much greater outcome toward goal setting and accomplishment when they are written down. Putting goals on paper also avoids a later misunderstanding and increases the level of commitment by becoming a *priority* with printed expectations.

Consider that it was Bishop Fulton J. Sheen who said this about reaching out toward to our goals. "When we walk toward the light, the shadow will always follow, but when we walk away from the light, the shadow is always in front of us."

YOUR LEADERSHIP VISION

Perhaps the most important quality that sets a leader apart from a mere manager is the ability to construct and articulate a vision. Leaders use vision to establish and interpret a hopeful image of the future. This visual picture must be persuasive, attractive and desirable to everyone on the team. The need for vision is important for organizations, group activities and family relationships. Leadership is enhanced by the ability to visualize both the challenges of today and the aspirations and hopes of a better tomorrow. To be most effective, this vision needs to be communicated so clearly that everyone is able to mentally grasp it and picture themselves *living* in that future. The vision needs to be possible and believable, but it also needs to be challenging and have an unrestricted feel to it. For example, a part of the Microsoft® Corporation's vision has been "a computer on every desk and in every home."

Providing vision is *always* an important need for a leader. However, it is even more important during times of crisis or stress. During times of great difficulty, people especially need a positive vision of meaning and hope. When either an individual or an organization is in a state of confusion and in despair, they are most receptive to an optimistic illustration of a mission or purpose! How can leaders provide this kind of a visionary message? It is only possible to those who take the time and effort to discover the most fervent desires and deepest values of their supporters. Experienced leaders realize there is more than a single desire and value to be discovered. In reality, the future often announces itself from afar. For most, the noisy clutter of today drowns out the timid sounds of events to come. For the leader, focused attention on these weak timid sounds provides the seeds of vision for a better tomorrow. When communicated clearly, a vision helps people to overcome their perceived defensive positions and self-limitations to discover something bigger than themselves. It inspires them to desire membership within a group and to accept a degree of self-sacrifice. I believe author and management consultant Peter Block defines *vision* in a majestic way as:

"Our deepest expression of what we want. It is the preferred future, a desirable state, an ideal state, an expression of optimism. It expresses the spiritual and idealistic side of human nature. It is a dream created in our waking hours of how we would like our lives to be."

In the past, an organization's vision was typically developed and established by a single individual such as the president or CEO. A single leader exclusively created a vision and then persuaded others to accept it. In recent times, many are now seeing the wisdom of developing a vision that incorporates the aspirations of more than one individual or a small elite group of individuals. In our modern cultural climate, no amount of oratory skill or personal charisma can sell a limited vision that reflects only one leader's views. Vision isn't about wildly claiming to know the future. It is about *discovering* the hopes and dreams of a better tomorrow and providing the picturesque motivation to get there. Leadership also recognizes that even the seeds of imperfectly formed images expressed by others can help create a *new* vision.

Once a vision is clearly established, how does the leader convey the mission and inspire others onward? Most people would say the answer is to provide stirring oratory or charisma. Yet these powerful tools are *not* absolutely necessary for visionary leadership. For example, Thomas Jefferson was a poor orator and public speaker. Yet he used his polished *writing* skills and personal warmth to motivate others. Other powerful tools include the use of symbols and stories to communicate a vision. A leader can frame a *common experience* that followers can all *relate* to. The famous "I Have a Dream" speech by Martin Luther King framed the experience of the March on Washington in 1963 to his followers. King framed the event by inspiring his listeners to feel that history was being made in their very presence.

Another recognized way for the leader to communicate vision is to express it as often as possible with vivid imagery that includes slogans or colorful emotional language. Take the time to explain just how the vision can be achieved and exhibit a personal example of optimism and confidence. As others move toward acceptance of the vision, express confidence in their attitudes and skills. Catch them doing something well and help them to develop self-confidence. As a leader, remember to *celebrate* the successes and milestones of achievement toward the vision. This helps to generate enthusiasm and excitement since everyone appreciates recognition and rewards.

Finally, as a leader you must lead by personal example, modeling the values you expect of others. Nothing *erodes* a vision more quickly than a hypocritical leader who violates expected standards and values. Your example should also include giving others the authority and empowerment they need to do their jobs. Remember, empowering means to provide the resources others need to carry out the tasks assigned to them.

In conclusion, consider the importance of your own *personal* vision. Outside of the business world we also need to maintain a vision within our *families* and our personal lives. Take the time to ponder your own personal vision! Write it down as your very own mission statement and refer to it often. As an individual it will give you the optimistic inspiration for a better tomorrow and it will provide *you* with a greater sense of purpose and meaning.

Consider that it was Martin Tupper who once said, "It is sure to be dark, if you shut your eyes!"

WHAT ARE YOUR VALUES?

Organizational values are the *guiding principles* that state how the employees, beginning with management, intend to conduct their behavior and do business. These values will determine what kind of a company will develop and become the foundation of the organizations culture. They become an important part of individuality for both the organization and individuals! Values deal with preferences, perceptions, judgments and behavior. This belief system has a *profound* influence on the way employees communicate and interact with each other.

Many businesses articulate a set of values to emphasize their own distinctiveness or drive their competitive advantage. On an organizational level, these values should include a respect for all of the stakeholders. In addition to these values, the willingness to support the *need* for change or renewal within the organization is important.

Some leaders have viewed their values as contingent upon the situation or their immediate needs. This is a recipe for long-term disaster! In reality, effective leadership is *not* based on the contingency of times or circumstances but on the most fundamental of *moral* values—respect for people. In this essential ethical value, there is no room for contingencies. Trust is the emotional *glue* that bonds leaders and followers together. When followers feel manipulated or treated dishonestly, they cease being committed supporters and become resistant.

Value-based leadership is a philosophy and attitude about people and processes. It is founded on integrity, open communication, respect, feedback and ethical behavior. The hearts and minds of followers are energized by inclusion and participation. Leadership should provide a durable and persuasive sense of purpose and direction. It recognizes that in order for an organization to overcome resistance to change, the leaders must start by changing themselves! In this way the leader inspires others to join and lead in the transformation. When this occurs, one becomes, in the words of James O'Toole, a "leader of leaders."

Here are some of the qualities of a value-based leader...

- A demonstration of professionalism.

- Acts in accordance with organizational values.

- Actively supports and promotes company values.

- Introduces values to new associates and followers.

- Views oneself as a role model for company and personal values.

Don't overlook or underestimate the importance and influence of values. The right values will mean commitment, balance and the ability to accept change. The wrong values will mean coercion, instability and resistance to needed change.

Consider that it was Seneca who once said, "If a man does not know what port he is steering for, no wind is favorable to him."

COMMITMENT

What leaders want and need from others is commitment. This is one's emotional investment to extend great effort toward the implementation of a decision, outcome or goal. Successful leaders need to solicit the commitment and dedication of others to achieve established goals and the group's mission. Just how does a leader build commitment among followers and various stakeholders? A number of vital keys are important. I will list *five* valuable points.

1. *Gaining commitment from others is no longer considered a right or obligation.* As many leaders painfully learn, you can't buy commitment from others no matter how much you pay them. Commitment is a building process and it is *earned* by a leader who appreciates and values it!

2. *The enemy of commitment is silence and exclusiveness demonstrated by the leader.* Building commitment means open and honest communication. A wise leader understands that most individuals have a natural resistance to change and are suspicious of any idea or concept *forced* upon them. Commitment is enhanced when the genuine *need* for change is clearly and patiently expressed and when the followers' input is respected as part of the entire change process.

3. *The friend of commitment is involvement.* People feel a greater sense of commitment when they are involved in the decision-making process. Many leaders fear this because they are afraid that others may offer other options or challenge their own thinking. Experienced leaders don't fear seeking the involvement of followers because they understand the deepened level of commitment far outweighs the potential of a compromised decision. They know that even the most sound and brilliant decision will *fail* without the commitment of others.

4. *Ask for the commitment of others.* This can be done by vividly articulating a clear vision, and *personally* requesting their solid commitment. Don't take the support of other workers for granted! Let them know how important they are and how vital their commitment is to achieve success. Often times a personal

plea will make a big difference in gaining the deep commitment of others.

5. *Set an individual example by demonstrating your own level of commitment.* Show others that you are willing to do what you ask of them. Commitment is easily eroded by leaders who think they are "above" and "beyond" the tasks expected of others. In contrast, leaders who will roll up their sleeves and occasionally share some lower tasks with others win the respect and admiration of followers. By doing this you state to the follower that you value what they do and appreciate their valuable contribution to the organization.

In conclusion, commitment and involving others in the *entire* decision-making process creates an emotional bond. Use open and honest communication to express the need and reasons for change. Deeply involve the followers to help determine how the change should occur. In exchange for their inclusion, ask for commitment as their promise of dedication and support. Commitment is founded on trust, respect and a common vision.

Consider that it was Peter Block who wrote, "People engaged in the redesign of their governance need to commit to act in the interests of the whole organization. Freedom and commitment are in every case joined at the hip."

WHAT IS YOUR REAL MOTIVE TO LEAD?

The personal desire to lead others is often a powerful and compelling urge. However, whether you will be an effective leader and produce positive long-term results depends on your *real motive* to lead others! The ability to get things accomplished and influence people is often defined as *power*. Many individuals have a strong *internal* need for power and research shows that these individuals typically seek positions of authority in organizations. People with a low need for power characteristically lack the assertiveness and desire to advocate change or manage others well. The aspiration to lead others and seek power can be a positive or negative event depending on your motivation. Researchers like David C. McClelland have also established *two* different types of motives found in individuals to indicate their intention to seek power. One type is called *personalized power orientation* and the other is referred to as *socialized power orientation*. Certainly most leaders will fall somewhere in between these two power orientations rather than be exclusively one or the other.

Those with a *personalized power orientation* seek to gain power to inflate themselves and satisfy their strong need for esteem and status from others. They tend to exercise power impulsively and have little inhibition and self-control. They seek to *dominate* others by keeping them weak and dependent. They desire to collect symbols of prestige such as "big offices" and impressively priced automobiles. All authority to make important decisions is centered around them and they use rewards or punishments to control and manipulate others. Individuals with a personalized power orientation are often rude and demanding.

The culture of an organization with a personalized power orientation has a *restricted* communication flow. Followers are slow to show initiative or to solve problems. Instead they wait for direct instructions from the leader. Little talent is developed within the followers since the fear of infringing on the leader's authority is always present. Any loyalty exhibited from the followers is likely to be toward the leader *only* and not to the organization or its goals and vision. When the leader departs, there will likely be disorder and a breakdown in functions.

Leaders with a *socialized power orientation* desire power for the *benefit* of others. Being human, they are by no means perfect, but they are far less egotistical, defensive and materialistic. They are more emotionally mature and respectful of others. Their strong desire for power is to *build up* an organization or others to be successful. They oppose the manipulation of others and only use their formal authority as a "last resort" if other positive ways to influence followers are not effective. They tend to use more of a *participative* "coaching style" of behavior and freely listen to advice from others. Those at the top of this orientation are often referred to as *servant leaders*.

The culture of an organization with a socialized power oriented leader has a better communication flow! Followers show *initiative* to solve problems more quickly since the leader has encouraged them to take action. Talent is more fully developed since learning is encouraged and valued at all levels. The loyalty exhibited from followers is likely to be for both the leader they respect, and the goals and vision of the organization. When the leader departs, the organization remains cohesive and continues to function well.

Now analyze *yourself* and your own leadership skills! What is *your* real motive to lead?

Consider that it was Henry Ward Beecher who wrote the following quote regarding leadership, "Greatness lies not only in being strong, but in the right use of strength."

Chapter 2

LEARNING TO SERVE BEFORE YOU LEAD

If you want to be a great leader who influences others and leaves a powerful legacy, you will need to transcend selfish motives and learn to serve others first. This service toward others will prepare you for future opportunities.

THE SERVANT LEADER APPROACH

Traditionally, almost all leaders have established and nurtured autocratic hierarchal organizations. Since the beginning of human civilization, certain individuals arose to assume positions of leadership among others. Leadership was often demonstrated by a "command and control" philosophy that sought to achieve only the leader's personal goals. Governments and military institutions gravitated toward this type of authoritarian leadership. This philosophical approach typically viewed followers simply as individuals to be controlled, manipulated and often disposable in order to achieve the leader's purposes. There was virtually no concern about the individual needs of followers. The reward offered to followers was continued survival, and possible advancement within the hierarchy if absolute loyalty was demonstrated.

With this historical background it is no surprise that an autocratic leadership approach was naturally followed during the birth of the Industrial Revolution. The changes brought by the Industrial Revolution of the eighteenth century overturned not only traditional economies, but also whole societies. Economic changes caused far-reaching social changes, including the movement of people to cities, and new ways of working. The Industrial Revolution was the first step in modern economic growth and development.

As the Industrial Revolution began, workers living in the cities and arriving from rural farms were often uneducated and unskilled for this new kind of labor. Work conditions were crude and the daily work hours demanded of them were oppressive. However, work was scarce and even meager wages could make the difference between survival or starvation. The emerging class of powerful business leaders viewed workers as basically ignorant, lazy, and undisciplined. Organizational leaders felt they must control and rigidly supervise all workers to maintain high levels of production. Business owners viewed themselves as paternalistic "father figures" who needed to dominate their "worker children." Workers who did not completely yield or conform to the owner's dictates were immediately terminated.

Eventually workers created labor unions to provide a counter-balance to this tyrannical approach and harsh treatment. For over 200 years the general approach of leadership was hierarchal and authoritarian. This began to change in the latter part of the twentieth century. Democratic institutions brought about greater choices for workers. Public education created an educated workforce with the knowledge and skills to compete for better jobs and opportunities. Workers along with their culture began to reject dictatorial hierarchal organizations and the treatment they received from them.

Robert K. Greenleaf spent his first career in management research and education at AT&T. He then began a second career teaching and consulting at various institutions, including the Harvard Business School, Ford Foundation, and scores of not-for-profit institutions. Greenleaf was perplexed by the tumultuous changing culture of the 1960's and sought to understand why so many young people were in rebellion against America's established organizations, especially educational institutions. He determined that the fault lie with the institutions; they were not doing a good job of serving! Therefore, he concluded they were doing a poor job of leading.

In 1970, Greenleaf wrote a small essay called *The Servant As Leader*, which introduced the term "servant leadership." In it, he described some of the characteristics and qualities of servant leaders. He included examples which showed that individual efforts, inspired both by "vision" and a servant attitude philosophy, can make a substantial difference in the quality of a society. Greenleaf wrote that true leaders are chosen by their followers. He discussed the skills necessary to become a servant leader; the importance of keen awareness, foresight and listening. Greenleaf clearly drew contrasts between servant leadership and the typical use of coercive, manipulative, and persuasive power. His later writings challenged conventional wisdom about hierarchical organization and the use of power in major modern institutions. Until his death in 1990, Greenleaf kept writing on the themes of management, power, servanthood, and spirituality.

Robert Greenleaf is considered the "father" of the modern servant leadership philosophy. However, this philosophy has existed for thousands of years and has been used effectively in various institutions, including religious organizations, for many centuries. Greenleaf simply defined and articulated it effectively for a new generation and culture. You can find out more about Robert Greenleaf and the organization he founded (*Greenleaf Center for Servant-Leadership*) at www.greenleaf.org.

Servant leadership is a positive philosophy that personifies people who choose to serve first, and then desire to lead as a way of expanding service to institutions and individuals. It encourages trust, collaboration, foresight, listening, and the ethical use of power. It is now part of the culture of many profitable and influential organizations including some mentioned in Fortune Magazine's annual "100 Best Companies To Work For" list. Servant leaders often hold no formal leadership positions or titles.

Perhaps I can provide no better definition than the one provided by Robert Greenleaf himself in his book, *The Servant As Leader*, originally published in 1970.

> "The servant leader is servant first... It begins with the natural feeling that one wants to serve, to serve first. Then conscious choice brings one to aspire to lead. He or she is sharply different from the person who is leader first, perhaps because of the need to assuage an unusual power drive or to acquire material possessions. For such it will be a later choice to serve – after leadership is established. The leader-first and the servant-first are two extreme types. Between them there are shadings and blends that are part of the infinite variety of human nature. The difference manifest itself in the care taken by the servant-first to make sure that other people's highest priority needs are being served. The best test, and difficult to administer, is: do those served grow as persons; do they, while being served, become healthier, wiser, freer, more autonomous, more likely themselves to become servants? And, what is the effect on the least privileged in society; will they benefit, or, at least, will they not be further deprived?"

Think about the servant leadership approach and how it can change your impact and influence as a leader!

Consider that it was Joe Jaworski who wrote, "The ultimate aim of the servant leaders quest is to find the resources of character to meet his or her destiny – to find the wisdom and power to serve others."

BECOME A LEADERSHIP MENTOR

Over the past decade many organizations have initiated formal mentoring programs to develop managerial or leadership skills in individuals. Mentoring is a special relationship in which an experienced leader seeks to help a protégé with less experience. The mentor is typically a respected manager at a higher supervisory level, and a recognized leader. This mentor is usually not the immediate supervisor of the protégé. Mentorship is intended to be a unique association between these two individuals to promote the personal development of the trainee.

Research has shown that mentors provide two important functions for the protégé.

1. *A mentor can help facilitate the career of the trainee by providing sponsorship, protection, visibility and assignments to promote personal development.* Mentoring is also a skill that provides learning and direction during change or other stressful circumstances. This includes transitional situations such as the trainee's promotion, transfer or reassignment within the organization.

2. *A mentor provides a psychosocial role for the protégé within this relationship.* This consists of coaching, personal counseling, acceptance and encouragement. The mentorship role creates a positive nurturing environment that can benefit both the mentor and trainee. The mentor can receive greater job satisfaction, a deeper sense of personal fulfillment as a teacher, and the development of even greater leadership skills in the process. Some research has shown that mentoring can result in greater success and career advancement for the protégé.

However, mentoring is not always successful and some studies suggest that informal mentoring may be more successful than formal mentoring programs! These studies suggest that personality conflicts, lack of mentor commitment, age and gender differences were more likely to occur in formal programs that included assigned mentors. A formal program has a greater chance of success if it is structured to allow for voluntary participation, a flexible choice of protégés by the mentor, and by clarification of the expected roles of both mentors and trainees.

The *key* is to recognize that organizations should encourage and endorse mentoring programs! It is not essential for the programs to be either formal or informal to be successful, but it is important for the programs to be established and supported in order to nurture the next generation of leaders.

If your organization does not presently have a mentoring program, consider the advantages it may offer. Volunteer your services as a potential mentor. You will find the opportunity to teach others and share your experiences to be satisfying and enlightening. Here are some vital points to remember!

Show a genuine concern for the development of others— Encourage the trainee to establish their own individual goals and respond enthusiastically to their needs when you are approached.

*Help the protégé recognize their skill deficiencies—*There is often a gap between their existing skills and the required skills needed to get to the next level of their personal best. Kindly point out these needs in a tactful and positive way.

*Give opportunities for skill development—*Provide special "on the job" projects and assignments to promote new skills and opportunities for the trainee. Follow-up by providing personalized coaching to allow the protégé to learn from their failures and successes.

*Provide helpful personal advice—*Emphasize the benefits of training courses, workshops and advanced degree programs. Provide guidance on how to deal with career problems, and how to keep their lives in a healthy balance.

*Be a role model—*Individuals listen to people they respect and admire. They are more inclined to imitate examples of effective behavior and positive attitudes. Remember that they are watching closely to see how you respond to highly difficult or challenging situations!

Consider that it was Bruce Barton who wrote, "When you are through changing, you're through."

WHAT IS "REVERSE MENTORING"?

For well over a decade, organizations have been encouraged to institute formal mentoring programs! In these programs, the senior and more experienced managers spend time with less experienced individuals to accelerate their learning concerning job skills, values and the organizational culture. In this environment, the senior managers often become role models for the younger or less experienced generation.

However, this may not be the only effective form of mentoring! While the traditional model works well for most organizations and can be a powerful tool to develop the future leaders of an organization. Another credible form of mentoring is called *reverse mentoring* or backward learning. In this arrangement, the younger or less experienced juniors, or "newbies", mentor certain skills, attitudes or perceptions to the senior members. They are given an "open forum" to provide fresh views or perspectives of the existing organization as they see it. Reverse mentoring is a bottom up approach rather than the traditional top down mentoring approach.

Here are just a few examples for you to consider. Former *General Electric* Chairman Jack Welch used reverse mentoring in 1999 when he directed 600 of his top managers to pair with younger workers to learn more about technology and the Internet. Other successful organizations, such as *Procter & Gamble*, have also used reverse mentoring as a successful strategy.

What are the benefits of reverse mentoring?

1. *An organization's culture should be constantly evolving for the better.* It must be flexible enough to adapt to higher standards and new ways to increase learning. Over time, senior leaders simply adopt and accept an existing culture. They mentally establish certain assumptions and typically only listen to those who are at the top of the organization's hierarchy. Though this can provide a sense of stability and continuity, it can also "choke off" or stunt needed self-analysis or examination in a rapidly changing environment or marketplace.

2. *Reverse mentoring sends the message to the less*

experienced members that their opinions and ideas are valued and really matter. Even if many of their opinions are not adopted, they at least know that they had the opportunity to candidly express their views. This promotes a deeper sense of commitment and "buy-in" toward various corporate strategies. This experience also helps the newbies to more quickly develop coaching, counseling, communication and mentoring skills.

3. *Senior members really can learn a lot from junior or less experienced members of the organization!* Each generation has its own unique strengths and weaknesses, and we can all learn from one another. The newcomers to an organization usually have only a brief period when they can offer fresh approaches, insights, and ideas to senior management. This is an excellent time to tap into their alternative perspectives before they slowly lose these qualities and become merged into the existing culture.

4. *Reverse mentoring can only be effective when senior managers are teachable and humble about the process.* They must temporarily set aside the subordinate-boss relationship and be willing to learn and question with an open mind. If this environment exists, the senior managers will be able to develop greater self-awareness, examine some obsolete assumptions and expand their technical skills. Again, this is only possible when the senior managers have an unassuming mind-set about the purpose and benefits of reverse mentoring.

Reverse mentoring can be an important and effective tool to validate or change an existing culture. Not all ideas, perspectives, opinions or insights provided by the less experienced members will be valid or legitimate. Perhaps most of them will not be embraced, but many of them will be beneficial and offer the opportunity for the corporate culture to change for the better!

Consider that it was Sam Rayburn who said, "You cannot be a leader and ask other people to follow you, unless you know how to follow, too."

BEING A LEADER AND A COACH

One of the most important roles of a modern leader is to be that of a coach. By definition a coach is a tutor who trains and motivates others to reach their greatest potential. In the past, many leaders acted more like coaches of athletes by shouting and intimidating others into action. This began to change in the late 20th century as it became evident that autocratic leadership no longer works in today's society and culture. It is true that autocratic leadership is effective and still valued in emergency or crisis situations. A recent example of this is the former mayor of New York City who was vilified for his autocratic leadership before September 11th, 2001 and lauded for it during a time of national crisis.

But the fact remains that autocratic leadership is no longer effective for the day-to-day activities of a healthy organization. People will simply not respond in effective or productive ways. The type of coaching required by today's leader is more like that of an orchestra conductor or an acting coach. The goal is to recognize and respect the individual skills inherent within each person. This is done by a combination of mutual respect, personal example, valuable tutoring, tactful correction, generous praise, continuous improvement and positive motivation skills.

This type of coaching is only possible from a leader who has the right approach and understanding of what it now means to be in a leadership position. This is a leader who desires to *build up* their subordinates and considers the development and success of others as their greatest achievement. This type of coaching is based on a philosophy of teaching and imparting knowledge and skills to others. There is no room for the need to control, manipulate, intimidate or demean others. Here is how you can become a coaching leader...

Lead by example—People will want to emulate you if they truly respect you. On the other hand, they will withdraw emotionally if your persona or actions lack credibility. Be approachable and earn a reputation as one who is always willing to supportively listen and help others to grow and develop.

Prompt others to analyze their performance—Begin by inviting others to do their own self-assessment before you comment. They may be aware of some of their own personal weaknesses and will be less defensive if they can express them rather than being told by you. In circumstances where they are not aware of perceived weaknesses, don't focus only on the weakness, but on helping them diagnose the reasons for mistakes and problems.

Build up their confidence and self-reliance—It is far better to influence others to finds ways to improve themselves rather than dictate commands about what you feel needs to be done. Ask the individual to explain what they have determined needs to be improved in themselves. Reinforce what they have discovered with positive comments and support. As a final task point out a single area of weakness they may not have discovered. Diplomatically provide an recent example of how this weakness was demonstrated and ask them how the same situation could be handled differently in the future. Take a few minutes to "role play" and model how the same situation can produce better results. Encourage them by explaining how you have struggled with similar difficulties and eventually mastered the problem. Finish the discussion by letting them know you have confidence in their ability to overcome a problem or learn a new skill.

Be there—Be more than "the boss" or a mentor. Also become a friend by allowing others to communicate with you in confidence without fear of reprisal or ridicule. Be patient as they vent their frustrations or criticisms. As an active listener hear them out and gently point out the flaws in their reasoning. Inspire them to become part of the solution to any difficulty and not part of the problem. Finally, remind them that their personal success is one of your most important goals.

Consider that it was Margaret Fuller who wrote, "If you have knowledge, let others light their candles at it."

LEADERSHIP AND TRUST

Trust is the glue that makes effective leadership possible. The *American Heritage Dictionary* defines trust as a "firm reliance on the integrity, ability, or character of a person or thing." Another definition given is "the condition and resulting obligation of having confidence placed in another." Without this bond of trust present in a culture, leadership is replaced by mere formal autocratic power. The head of one nation in our present world controls his people with so little trust that he regularly executes his closest generals and replaces them with a new generation of subordinates. They only survive until he feels suspicious of their loyalty or talents. Thankfully this is an extreme example but it reveals a dysfunctional environment permeated by mistrust.

Coworkers initially give trust to a leader as deference to their role or position. However, this is not always true if other past leaders or individuals manipulated them! The fact is that a leader must build trust within the group and continually rebuild this essential quality. It is a mistake to take it for granted. How can a leader build trust? Here are a few points to ponder...

Be truthful—This may seem obvious but unfortunately many leaders forget the importance of this quality. Being untruthful may work for a while but eventually others will lose respect for you. Both trust and truth are built upon the same ethical foundation of integrity. You must be perceived as someone who tells the truth even if it is sometimes difficult to express. Most individuals will be more accepting of learning something they "don't want to hear" from you than finding out you lied to them! This includes you being considered fair and objective towards others in difficult situations.

Be open—Keep people informed as to what you are thinking. Ask for their input and explain the rationale behind your decisions. Mistrust often comes from what people don't know more than from what they do know. If others perceive or learn that you are hiding information from them, you will be branded as deceitful and secretive. Be candid about problems and disclose relevant information you have. If asked to reveal information you hold in confidence about another, it is best to say you cannot violate a confidence rather than deny or lie about the knowledge you have. Obviously there is a need to balance being "open" in contrast to being told things in confidence by others. When you are being told things in confidence about other people or situations, you must maintain careful discretion with this information. Remember that others make themselves vulnerable by providing this information to you. They need to feel confident that you will not discuss it with others and betray their trust in you.

Be a promise keeper—Others listen to you more carefully than you realize. When you make a promise, other coworkers need to see you are dependable. As the old saying goes, "promises made must be promises kept." To maintain trust, you must keep your word and obligations. What about the rare situation where due to unforeseen circumstances the original promise you made cannot be kept? Don't simply ignore the original promise or pretend you never made it! Acknowledge you made the promise, explain why you are unable to keep it at this time, and offer to fulfill it when the right time or situation allows. Trust includes being consistent about the way you act and maintaining predictable behavior rather than irrational behavior.

Be sensitive—Showing others you care and expressing mature emotions helps to build trust. If you present only hard facts you will come across to others as aloof and cold. Respect for you will increase when people see you are a real person and have human sensitivities toward their needs.

Be competent—People naturally respect competent in-dividuals. Demonstrate your technical and professional skills and you will earn the admiration of others as a leader. Be sure to develop your interpersonal and communication skills. Coworkers feel good about working with competent, caring leaders and are more apt to trust them.

Consider that it was Peter Block who wrote, "Trust comes out of the experience of pursuing what is true."

MOTIVATING OTHERS

Motivating others is at the heart of leadership and organizational success. Before we discuss the topic of motivation, we need to understand the proper symbiotic relationship between people and organizations. First of all, organizations should exist to serve human needs and not the other way around. Organizations and people need each other. Employees need careers, opportunities, satisfaction and fulfilling work. Organizations need the energy, ideas and talent of its people. When the environment between the organization and individual is poor, one or both will suffer and become victims! The eventual result will be that either certain individuals will be exploited or they will exploit the organization.

With this foundation in mind we can see that leaders seek to nurture an organizational culture where work is productive, energizing and mutually rewarding. Psychologist Abraham Maslow created an influential theory to group human needs into five basic categories. These needs are hierarchical and begin with lower or basic needs. As these lower needs are met and satisfied, individuals are motivated by higher needs. The five basic categories begin with physiological needs like water, food, air and physical health. As this need is achieved an individual would seek a higher need for safety from danger or threat. Next is the need for belonging and love through personal relationships with other people. As this need is met one is then motivated by esteem, the feeling of being valued and respected. Finally, Maslow defined the highest need as self-actualization or the need to develop oneself to our fullest potential. Since Maslow published his "hierarchy of needs," others have also introduced various theories to explain human needs. All of these theories confirm the complex nature of human motivation.

Researcher Chris Argyris discovered a basic conflict between human personality and the way typical organizations are managed and structured. He determined that managers or bosses tend to control people at the lower levels and this produces dependence and passivity, which are in conflict with the real needs of human beings. Many organizations attempt to restrain workers through the creation of mechanized jobs, tight controls and more directives resulting in frustration. Argyris identified *six* ways workers respond to these frustrations.

1. They withdraw...through chronic absenteeism or simply by quitting.

2. They stay on the job but psychologically withdraw by becoming passive, indifferent and apathetic.

3. They resist by reducing output, or by deception, sabotage or featherbedding.

4. They try to climb the hierarchy to escape to a better job.

5. They form groups like labor unions to redress a power imbalance.

6. They socialize their children to believe that work is unrewarding and opportunities for advancement are slim.

Many of us have personally experienced or felt at least some of these frustrations. So what is motivation? It is the ability to provide an incentive or reason to compel others into action or a commitment.

How can a leader motivate others? It starts with the core value that employees are an investment and not a cost. The old model of management was that people are basically lazy, passive, have little ambition, resist change and must be treated like children. This dysfunctional management approach created generations of frustrated workers who reacted and worked exactly like they were treated. The leadership model of management realizes that people are the most valuable resource of an organization and typically its greatest untapped resource!

With this basic value, leaders establish a philosophy of an enhanced human resource strategy. They seek to hire the right people and reward them well. They provide a reasonable sense of job security, promote from within the organization whenever possible, budget generously to train and educate workers, share the wealth of the organization, and provide autonomy and participation. However, there is still one unique trait that sets leaders apart from others regarding human motivation.

Leaders recognize that a "one size fits all" approach does not work in motivating most workers. Each person has individual and personal needs. When these are discovered and fulfilled, the human potential of each worker can be maximized.

For example, some individuals are primarily motivated by money, though this has proven to be a short-term motivator. Others are motivated by being part of a team or something bigger than themselves. Others are motivated by continual challenge. Others need constant praise. The point is that all people are different and your leadership goal should be to help each individual to meet their own needs as well as the organizations needs. In reality, helping individuals achieve their personal needs is the most powerful motivator and will result in successful organizational accomplishment. A leadership perspective recognizes the personal contribution of each worker as a source of his or her highest motivation. Each individual has enormous creative power and is a steward of change, problem solving and progress. The very first step in motivating others is to give them respect, dignity and praise for their efforts!

Consider that it was Eleanor Roosevelt who once said, "When you cease to make a contribution, you begin to die."

THE ART OF FOLLOWERSHIP

L eaders can only exist and accomplish extraordinary goals because they have supportive followers! Both need each other to achieve the group's vision and established mission. Unfortunately, the term "to follow" or "follower" has gained a negative connotation in western society. Some sneeringly use the epithet "follower" to label an individual as one who is passive, inferior or without creativity. Yet, nothing could be further from the truth. Followers make things happen and thereby gain the valuable skills needed to grow themselves into leadership positions. Ira Chaleff, author of *The Courageous Follower: Standing Up to and for Our Leaders*, correctly argues that it is essential for our culture to change this negative perception of followers into a positive evaluation.

In the study of leadership theory, the word followership often defines those who acknowledge the central leader(s) as a source for guidance, motivation and authority. However, to a certain degree, all individuals are leaders and all are followers. Everyone in the modern workplace shares in at least some leadership role or responsibility and even a CEO may demonstrate followership within a relationship with the board of directors!

A team of knowledgeable and motivated followers can result in all necessary work being performed successfully. It rests upon the followers to complete most everyday jobs, maintain cooperative working relationships, share in various leadership functions and support the development of present and future leaders. Effective followers are an essential element in any group's success. They recognize that all leaders have strengths and weaknesses. Effective followers *help* the leader to fully utilize strengths and compensate or overcome the weaknesses. Followers provide constructive disagreement that helps to balance a leader's extremes. For example, the same fine leadership qualities that help a leader to be passionate, self-confident and a person of strong opinions may also contribute to the leader acting self-righteously, being overly ambitious and making serious high-risk decisions. Skillful followers who have developed a high level of respect and mutual trust with the leader are able to risk the leader's displeasure by offering a balanced or differing perspective. An important role within good followership is not to simply complain about the leader, but to help them to become a better leader.

What if your organization has weak or poor leadership? Sadly, this is a common problem today in most organizations. Many formal leaders with majestic titles lack either the desire or basic skills required for genuine leadership. However, effective followers can look beyond the present leadership void by having a strong commitment to the group or organization and its mission. Actually, mentoring a weak leader has side benefits for the dedicated follower. In assisting a weak leader, the follower will also develop and learn critical leadership skills.

It is *important* to remember that today's followers will become tomorrow's leaders! For instance, most people would look upon the accomplishments of Thomas Jefferson and immediately recognize his effective multifaceted leadership skills. However, in 1776 and at the age of 33, Jefferson played a follower's role as part of a committee established to create the *United States Declaration of Independence*. Dwarfed by other powerful committee members such as Benjamin Franklin and John Adams, he quietly drafted the document as a junior member of the committee. His authorship was little known outside of the Continental Congress and he received no public recognition until eight years afterward when it was revealed in a newspaper article. This significant contribution of a follower helped to change world history and the experience he gained from observing his senior committee members prepared him for *future* leadership responsibilities.

In the next two tips I will discuss some of the individual qualities of good followership!

Consider that it was John Maxwell who has stated, "If you think you are leading and no one is following, you are only taking a walk!"

GOOD FOLLOWERSHIP QUALITIES – PART 1

We will now discuss some of the individual qualities of good *followership*. These qualities help the follower to be more effective and prepare them for future positions of leadership. Learning to serve and follow others helps one to develop the empathy and humility needed for superb leadership. These followership guidelines are based on taking personal responsibility, maintaining trust and credibility and remaining true to your deeply felt convictions.

Know what you are expected to do. You cannot appear to be reliable and competent if your role is vague or ambiguous. Make sure your job tasks have been clearly communicated to you by the leader(s). What are your responsibilities, performance standards, and range of authority? Establish and maintain contact with your leader to minimize inconsistent or unclear messages. Your first major task is to be diplomatic but fervent to resolve any ambiguity or conflict about your role with the leader. You can only be a successful and beneficial follower if both you and the leader know exactly what your tasks are and what boundaries you have to achieve them.

Take initiative and keep the leader informed. You are expected to take the personal initiative to solve problems that block the achievement of goals and objectives. This initiative may take different forms including solving the problem yourself, pointing out difficulties to others and suggesting ways to solve various problems. There may be times when it is expedient to initiate a "pilot project" to prove the validity of an idea or different approach before presenting the concept to the leader. It is also important to keep the leader informed about the important actions and decisions you are making. It is embarrassing to a leader to find out from others what you are doing and why! Mutual trust and respect is built upon good communication and positive relationships.

Provide accurate information and feedback. Good followers know it is their responsibility to provide clear and accurate information to their leader. In reality, the follower has extensive power over what the leader knows and this may positively or negatively affect the quality of their decisions. Good decisions are based on timely and sound information. Your responsibility is to relay both good news and bad news. A leader will not respect or appreciate distorted or erroneous information provided by a follower who has a "hidden agenda." Make sure you verify the information you receive, and if you cannot, be sure to acknowledge it as questionable or limited.

Support the leader's efforts to generate positive change. Lasting and productive change requires the cooperative effort of many individuals in an organization. It is a myth that a single heroic leader can initiate change. All change meets with resistance, and the leader needs support and encouragement during this time of additional stress. Offer to provide additional emotional and task support to a frustrated leader who may be struggling with an immediate crisis or may feel overwhelmed with organizational change.

Respectfully challenge the leader's flawed plans or strategies. This is perhaps the most valuable contribution of a loyal follower and the most difficult because it risks the displeasure of the leader! It helps if you have the right approach. Begin by expressing your respect for the leader and your desire to be a helpful associate and team member. Present your disagreement as an honest concern about the existing situation and the decisions that led up to it. Describe the problems in specific terms rather than vague concepts. Do not make this a personal attack or critique of the leader's skills or ability. If the leader is skeptical of your genuine concerns, suggest a broader discussion with other credible followers to encourage reconsideration of the original decision.

Ponder on these qualities over the next few days. How many do you presently possess? How are your followership skills at this point in time? For the next tip we will examine even *more* valuable qualities of good followership!

Consider that it was Robert Burton who wrote the following quote regarding followership; "I light my candle from their torches."

GOOD FOLLOWERSHIP QUALITIES – PART 2

In part 2 of *Good Followership Qualities*, we continue to discuss the traits that promote outstanding followership behavior. Remember that these are the skills that prepare one for future leadership roles. Now that you have digested the previous tip, we are ready to analyze a few more qualities.

Show appropriate recognition and appreciation of the leader(s). Leaders face a lot of pressure and bear many heavy responsibilities. They may often feel as if their efforts are unappreciated! Good followers are sensitive to the stresses and needs of the leader, and they provide encouragement and emotional support in a consistent and professional way. An appropriate balance is required, and this should not be confused with insincere brown-nosing, which is often used in a manipulative way simply to gain favor.

Provide "upward" counseling and coaching when necessary. Most people incorrectly look at leadership and followership from a limited and narrow perspective. They falsely believe that the leader does all the coaching and counseling directed toward followers. This may be true the majority of the time but certainly not exclusively. The leader may be new or inexperienced in their position and need the advice and experience offered by a follower. Sometimes the follower has greater expertise or more facts about a particular subject. Good followers are willing and able to provide upward coaching when appropriate. For more information, I encourage you to read *Leading Up, How To Lead Your Boss So You BOTH WIN* by Michael Useem.

Say no...when it is necessary! There are two things a good follower will absolutely not accept! This is abusive or unethical behavior demonstrated by the leader(s). One of the primary roles of the follower is to be the "conscience" of the organization. Leadership behavior that becomes abusive toward others or immoral is inexcusable. As a follower, it is important to challenge these flaws before they become habitual. In these situations it is acceptable to be diplomatic, yet firm with the leader. Point out the negative consequences of this inappropriate behavior and make it clear that you feel it is deplorable. A follower's loyalty and commitment to the leader must be weighed against established organizational and societal values.

Followership is an essential and effective "training ground" to prepare for future leadership opportunities. It requires balance, flexibility and a large degree of self-management. The experience gained from this role is often looked back upon as one of the most rewarding times in a leader's career.

Consider that it was Jules Ormont who wrote the following quote regarding leadership; "A great leader never sets himself above his followers except in carrying responsibilities."

UNDERSTANDING DIFFERENT NEEDS OF PEOPLE

Great leaders understand more than ever that different people working around them have different needs. In our diverse and global environment, the archaic attitude that everyone has the same needs (more money) no longer works and will ultimately drive an organization toward failure. The fact is that people come from various backgrounds, cultures, religious beliefs and personal experiences. These all have an effect on what motivates individuals and what becomes most important to them! Virtually all workers have the following needs, but they also have *specific ones* that matter most to them. Effective leaders take the time needed to truly know the people they work with to discover each individual's needs. Here is a list of the most important needs you will discover in your organization.

Equity—This is particularly important among younger workers. This individual wants to be treated fairly and equitably! They are likely to compare perks, work hours, salary and job duties between individuals who have the same basic job. Many female workers who do the same job as others but receive less pay are naturally sensitive to this important issue. They will become disillusioned if they see a lack of fairness and equity in the organization.

Achievement—This person receives personal satisfaction and fulfillment by getting things done. They want their job to be challenging so they can satisfy this deep need. The key for a leader is to give them stimulating duties and assignments so they can continue to meet their desire to accomplish tasks and projects.

Esteem—These are workers who crave personal praise and acknowledgement even more than a raise. Their need is to be told often that they are important and appreciated! When possible, take the time to give them public recognition and positive feedback on how they are doing. If this need is not met, their motivation and enthusiasm will decline rapidly.

Autonomy—For this person a feeling of independence and freedom is important. If trained properly, this individual typically works very well alone. If they have proven their competence and are diligent, consider allowing them the ability to set their own flexible schedule and to make many of their own choices or decisions. This doesn't mean teamwork on their part isn't important. Being part of the team is necessary and expected! It simply means they are primarily allowed to work in an independent environment where they thrive and meet their greatest need.

Affiliation—In contrast to those who desire independence, these workers thrive while interacting with others! They are highly social and enjoy working alongside fellow workers. They are motivated by more teamwork responsibilities like groups, committees, and projects. A leader can motivate them by giving these workers more opportunities to work and communicate with others to meet this important personal need.

Safety and Security—For these workers, a stable and secure workplace is their greatest need. These workers desire a steady salary and fringe benefits. Their most important needs (and primary motivator) are job security, a hazard free workplace, a predictable work routine and little risk of uncertainty in their environment. These are the true "worker bees" who do the basic daily duties that keep the organization working smoothly.

Power—This person has a deep-seated need to influence others and lead. They are often motivated by titles, position and power. If balanced and channeled in a positive direction, give them the opportunity to head committees, direct group projects and make independent decisions. These workers are often the next generation of leaders nurtured within the organization. As a leader, mentor them well and be sure to model and teach them excellent servant leadership principles!

Consider that it was Gene Fowler who said, "Men are not against you; they are merely for themselves."

GIVING THE RIGHT KIND OF PRAISE!

Many leaders know the value of providing praise to those who work with them. If used correctly, praise can be highly motivating and a great way to show someone you appreciate the good work they provide. But if a leader hands out praise for the wrong reasons, or at the wrong time, it can backfire and generate more harm than good. The key is to give the right kind of praise for the right reasons. Here are some guidelines to follow...

Don't casually praise mediocre performance. If you do this repeatedly, you reduce the impact and meaning of genuine praise. Also, when someone truly does excellent work, your praise will not mean very much. Another problem is that praising a co-worker for ordinary work won't necessarily motivate them to grow or perform even better. Don't confuse praise for showing appreciation. A leader should always show appreciation for all work others do, including a sincere "thank you"!

Be specific about what you are praising. Vague compliments like "keep up the good work" or "great job" are shallow. If the person just got done spending an hour making a personal phone call or eating a box of doughnuts, they will think you don't have a clue about their work habits! Providing fuzzy clichés only devalues genuine praise. Instead, make statements like, "I am impressed with the excellent work you did on the _____ project" or "the _____ problem." Again, be specific and let them know exactly what you found to be outstanding performance and why.

Skillfully use praise to improve poor performance. Most workers have both strong and weak skills. When a co-worker is performing well in one area and is weak in another, use praise to improve the weak area. Do this by taking the time needed to casually talk to the worker. In your conversation, praise what they are doing well and tell them why. Then encourage them to apply the same dedication and diligence to their weaker skills. Within the next few days, look for a reason to praise them in these weak areas as you see an effort to improve.

Put excellent praise in writing. Verbal praise can be very encouraging, but it can also be quickly forgotten when the next problem arises. Occasionally, provide genuine praise to others in the form of a memo or letter. It will be a permanent reminder to them of your admiration for their excellent work. When work related stresses later arise, it can be reread and encourage the reader all over again! Also, send a copy of the memo to the worker's supervisor and ask that it be placed in their personnel file. Believe me, this courtesy will mean a lot to the person being praised.

Don't assume praise is all that is needed. Over time superior work deserves more than praises and words of appreciation! If praise is not supported with other individual needs, it will eventually ring hollow. Don't forget to spend time with your workers! Aggressively work hard to get them occasional bonuses, raises, and job assignments they desire. Also, make it a point to take them out to lunch or dinner, on the company, as a way of showing your admiration for the work they do.

Be *generous* with giving genuine praise to others! Remember to use this powerful tool in the right way, and you will find it to be an effective motivator and a way to develop mutual respect.

Consider that it was William James who said, "The art of being wise is the art of knowing what to overlook."

ARE PEOPLE CAPABLE OF DOING MORE?

Are most workers capable of doing more in the workplace? What workers are saying about themselves may truly surprise you. According to a study by William M. Mercer, Inc., *twenty-five percent* of workers stated they were capable of performing *fifty percent* more work! Shockingly, all respondents estimated they could actually do *twenty-six percent* more work than they presently do.

So why don't they? Over thirty-three percent mentioned a lack of adequate training and good supervision. About thirty-three percent of those surveyed specifically mentioned one or more of the following *three* statements below. Their statement is followed by my own comments on why these are so harmful to morale and effectiveness. These problems are the direct result of *poor* leadership in an organization.

1. *The lack of a reward for good performance.* The right kind of reward for good performance is a strong motivator. It shows appreciation and recognition for a "job well done." For example, providing generic merit wages to all employees (whether they perform well or not) is an insult to high performers, and sends the message that good performance and poor performance are valued equally and rewarded evenly. A successful leader will find various and creative ways to reward those who excel and work effectively on the job. Remember that a reward does not always need to be monetary to be effective!

2. *Not being involved in decision-making.* This is a common problem in the workplace. Workers who are closest to the actual marketplace (and customers) are typically ignored and rarely consulted. On the other hand, individuals who are farther away from the customer or constituents tend to be the decision-makers. This is the end result of an ineffective hierarchy and managerial arrogance. Yes, it takes time and patience to solicit *input* and *ideas* from various workers who may not be either managers or articulate. But their experience and knowledge of the "trenches" is invaluable and will result in better decision-making. When employees are left out of the process, especially when a decision involves their work skills, it tells them they and

their ideas don't really matter. People who feel this way will not perform all the work they are fully capable of. Sound leaders learn how to tap into this powerful human resource and are able to greatly improve the quality of the decisions they make.

3. *No opportunity for advancement.* Imagine that you are an enthusiastic worker who has a deep desire to advance to another position within an organization. You receive rave reviews and are recognized as a good performer. Now imagine how you feel when a desirable position becomes open and someone is brought in from the "outside" to fill it! Also, imagine that you are not even considered or interviewed for the position. Unfortunately, this scenario happens thousands of times every day. It costs many organizations highly talented individuals who resentfully leave to pursue a career where they are appreciated and have opportunities for advancement. As a leader, it is essential for you to discover which employees have a strong desire for advancement and *find* ways to meet their needs. Recognizing and retaining talented people is essential to reach the organization's mission and achieve its vision.

Consider that Mark Twain once said, "Thunder is good, thunder is impressive; but it is lightening that does the work."

CAN MONEY BUY HAPPINESS?

A common *myth* in our society is that monetary affluence has a direct effect on our level of happiness. It has been said that "money can't buy happiness... but it makes a great down payment!" The truth as various facts and studies prove, is that an influx of money may bring a temporary rush of contentment. However, this achievement soon becomes a normal expectation and the rush quickly declines. Some economists call this "hedonic adaptation and social comparison." Once we receive the big raise or make a new purchase, it is rapidly accepted as a new standard and we want more.

Recent studies of multimillion-dollar lottery winners have shown that many developed negative lifestyle habits that brought a great degree of unhappiness. Also, a surprising number of them were bankrupt within a decade after they gained dollars that should have lasted a lifetime. *The National Opinion Research Center at the University of Chicago* has been studying this subject for many years. They report that the number of people defining themselves as "very happy" peaked at thirty-five percent in 1957. This has declined to thirty percent today even though Americans have achieved a dramatic increase in annual after tax income, and new technology has eased many burdens.

It is true that not having a job, or living in poverty can be discouraging and frustrating. In this case, securing a job with a generous salary can bring about increased happiness. Yet, many social scientists now understand that once we attain a certain income level that provides basic comfort, happiness is hardly increased at all by greater affluence! So if money alone can't buy happiness, what does contribute to personal contentment and a feeling of fulfillment? It appears that the basic philosophy of servant leadership has been right all along!

The prestigious *Case Western Reserve University* medical school has sponsored 21 scientific studies of human motivation, altruism, and compassionate behavior. In 2001 the university established *The Research on Unlimited Love* to answer the question of what does provide happiness. One common discovery is that happiness is not something you can attempt to gain for yourself or buy...it is a byproduct of helping others! It means taking your focus off yourself and sharing your time, talents, and finances to serve people. This understanding is the real *core* of all servant leadership principles.

Here are some thoughts on what really provides happiness...

1. *Realize that happiness that endures does not come from financial gain.* Yes, its complete absence brings misery but money doesn't guarantee you will be happy. In contrast, possessing a focus on obtaining money often becomes a formula for selfishness, anxiety and depression.

2. *Manage your time well and organize your life.* There is not enough time to do all the worthwhile things you desire, so it is important to determine your own priorities.

3. *Take care of your body and mind with regular exercise and balanced amount of sleep.* This is important for both our physical and mental well-being.

4. *Give the highest priority in life to developing and maintaining close personal relationships.* These relationships have the potential of bringing a high degree of love, happiness and contentment.

5. *Focus beyond yourself and be grateful for the things you do have in life.* Studies also show that people with a high degree of spirituality in their lives have a greater degree of happiness and self-fulfillment.

Consider that it was George Bernard Shaw who said, "Happiness is a perfume you cannot pour on others without getting a few drops on yourself."

Chapter 3

POSITIVE LEADERSHIP TRAITS

There are certain qualities that allow effective leaders to become high performers. Learning to manage your time and delegate unimportant activities is only the beginning. Inspiring others to become part of an innovative team that welcomes change will take your mission to the next level.

LEADERSHIP AND TIME MANAGEMENT – PART 1

Time Management is an important quality to a leader. What is time management? It is organizing our time to bring value and efficiency into the tasks we perform! It is not working more hours, or just harder, but more effectively. We are often rightly concerned about how we spend our money. Yet, we should also desire to *maximize* the worth of our time. By managing our time wisely, we can convert the minutes or hours now wasted during a normal business day into time that can be used more productively and effectively. We won't *regain* time by looking at large blocks of needed activity. We reclaim time by looking at small pieces of wasted effort! Here are some examples...

- *If you save 30 seconds every five minutes, by the end of the day you have saved an hour!*

- *By reclaiming 15 minutes a day, 7 days a week, you will retrieve an extra 2¼ working weeks per year!*

The first place to begin is by taking a serious analysis of how you spend each day. Purchase or create a "time analysis log" that reflects a typical 24 hour period on a work day. The log should have each hour of the day divided into 10 or 20 minute sections. To the right of the time divisions write down what you did the last 24 hours.

For example...

Time	Activity
8:00 AM	_____
8:10 AM	_____
8:20 AM	_____
8:30 AM	_____
8:40 AM	_____
8:50 AM	_____

This will help you to identify where your time goes every 24 hours during a typical week day. This self-analysis is much more effective if you perform this examination for an entire 7 day week! You may find that you are either wasting time, or using it poorly because of an acquired habit or mere convenience. Many people are surprised to discover how much time they spend in front of a television or in unproductive meetings. Look for ways you are wasting time or using it poorly. Are there activities you can change, consolidate or even eliminate? See how much time you can reclaim at home or at work by looking for the small pieces of wasted effort.

Another way we can begin to reclaim time is by knowing the difference between important and urgent. Important is defined as "of much significance or consequence." On the other hand, urgent is defined as "pressing; compelling or requiring immediate action or attention." Don't confuse "urgent" matters with what is really important, as it will consume your valuable time and effectiveness. People will often bring matters to you that they believe are urgent. The real question is...are they important? There is not enough time to do all the worthwhile things you desire and need to do! Therefore, an effective leader must focus on the high-value important activities. If you don't do this your entire day will be consumed with seemingly urgent, yet unimportant issues brought to your attention.

We often start out a day with the best of intentions, but then "problems" arise that seemingly must be solved now! This is often referred to as "crisis management." Some organizations have a dysfunctional culture that constantly operates in a crisis management mode. If you seem to be forced to confront this problem on a daily basis, it is difficult to manage your time effectively. Here are some things to consider...

1. *Schedule and complete your own work and projects before they become urgent and contribute to the problem.* Learn to control what you can control. This means not procrastinating and waiting to the last minute to get your own work done.

2. *Give yourself more time than you think you'll need to complete a task.* Most of us tend to underestimate the amount of time it will take to complete something we consider "easy", and to overestimate the "difficult" tasks.

3. *When faced with a large project, don't let it overwhelm you.* Break it down into smaller components (goals) and tackle them one by one. Start by simply collecting ideas and information by putting them in a new file.

4. *When something urgent "comes up" don't under react or overreact.* Give yourself a little time to think it through. A well thought out answer or decision is better than an impulsive one.

5. *You can schedule a block of time on your daily agenda to work on spontaneous urgent matters.* Very little happens that is actually life threatening. In most cases you can put off an urgent problem for at least a half hour or perhaps half a day. Acting instead of reacting to an urgent problem will result in better solutions.

For the *next* tip I will recommend a time management system that will help you to organize your life!

Consider that it was John Randolph who wrote, "Time is at once the most valuable and the most perishable of all our possessions."

LEADERSHIP AND TIME MANAGEMENT – PART 2

For this tip I recommend a time management system to help you *organize* your life and manage your time more effectively. By doing this, we will reclaim more time to demonstrate leadership in other vital ways. The key to achieving this higher level of organization is to establish a Master List, Master Calendar and Master File.

Let's begin by briefly mentioning your *Master List*. It keeps an inventory of all your unfinished work and ongoing projects. Anything that remains in progress or undone should be *written* on your Master List. Some people use a paper format and others use a software program, depending on their preference. Here are some things to include on your own Master List.

- Date the list, and update it daily.

- Use lined paper, either letter or legal sized.

- Write on each line. It is an itemized "to-do" inventory.

- When you finish a project, give yourself the pleasure of crossing off the item from the list.

- Keep it on top of the desk where you can see it.

- Each evening, closely review it and update it for tomorrow's priorities.

- Coordinate it with your Master Calendar.

Your *Master Calendar* is used in conjunction with your Master List, and together they help you to focus on what you have scheduled to do and what is really important. Here are some important qualities of your Master Calendar.

- It goes hand-in-hand with your Master List.

- On it are your scheduled appointments or meeting times transferred from your Master List.

- It should offer a daily and weekly calendar view.

- If your calendar is on a software program, print it out each day and keep it next to your Master List on your desk.

- Each evening, review and scan it for tomorrow's activities. Again, coordinate it with your Master List.

When daily information or potential new tasks arrive, you should quickly make one of the following decisions. First, if it concerns you, add it to your Master List. Secondly, if it concerns someone else or their job, pass it on. Third, if it is not important, quickly glance at it and throw it away! Now that we can focus on what is important as noted on our Master List, we can make sure our work space in not cluttered and confusing. To achieve this we create a Master File.

Your *Master File* is the collection of all separate file folders you individually create for each project or task on your Master List. Your Master File is kept in your desk drawer or in a file box. (Again, some individuals desire to use a paper format, and others may use a software program.)

All papers regarding a client, customer or a project should be kept together in a file folder. This includes reports, meeting notes, phone conversations, correspondence, etc. Remember to never put a piece of unfinished work inside a file folder without "noting it" on your Master List because you will forget it. Here are things to *heed* when maintaining your Master File.

- Write the name of the project or client on the folder tab. Label each folder clearly.

- Don't write small bits of information "on" a file folder itself. Use a separate piece of paper and place it inside.

- Keep all folders in a drawer and off your desk unless you are presently working on these specific projects.

- If you do this with software, use a good file manager like VCOM PowerDesk Pro®.

- Arrange folders in order of importance or frequency of use.

- Use staggered tabs. Different folder colors can indicate a different level of importance.

- Don't reuse old paper folders. You want them to look fresh, clean and professional.

If you do this diligently, your work environment will be uncluttered and functional. Here is a brief recap. All your ongoing projects are written on your Master List. Any items that are date sensitive are also coordinated on your Master Calendar. All information regarding your various projects are now located in a Master File. Inside it are the separate file folders for each of your projects. Keep the files you are not presently working on off your desk. It is essential to keep your work space clear and free from distraction.

When you complete a project, file it away and ~~cross it off~~ your Master List! By establishing and maintaining a Master List, Master Calendar and Master File system, you are well on your way to more effective time management!

Consider that it was Thomas Carlyle who wrote, "Do the duty that lies nearest thee; thy next duty will then become clearer."

THE ART OF DELEGATION – PART 1

One of the most important skills a leader can exercise is the right use of delegation. Some managers who are "control oriented" rarely delegate tasks. When they do delegate they closely monitor the results. They want to insure tasks are exactly performed the way they would do it! On the other hand, some managers delegate virtually all their own tasks in an effort to avoid work or responsibility. Between these two extremes is an effective balance! Proper delegation involves giving new and different tasks to individuals who report to you. It is a power sharing agreement where the delegator provides direction on the tasks involved, the magnitude of responsibilities given, and the range of discretion granted to make decisions without the delegator's approval. In this leadership tip we will discuss *what* tasks to delegate and in the next tip we will examine *how* to delegate tasks. Here are some ideas on what to delegate to others...

Delegate tasks that are not a high priority, but are considered urgent. Duties that need to get done quickly but are not highly important are good tasks to delegate. If you seem to have a number of urgent tasks, but never seem to have enough time to complete them, consider delegating them as an option. It is better for these duties to be completed on time and routinely by others, rather than be delayed or ignored by you.

Delegate tasks of suitable difficulty. Again, balance is the key with this point. Any task you delegate should be a challenge and difficult enough to encourage *new* learning skills. Allow some minor mistakes to occur as this is an important part of the learning process. However, don't delegate tasks that are "over" someone's head or potential skill level. It is not productive to give someone a responsibility that will result in failure and undermine their self-confidence.

Delegate tasks that can help challenge or develop another's career path. If you are preparing an individual to move into a specific role of greater responsibility, delegate to them tasks that are relevant to that future role. Perhaps you can make a delegated task part of a "new project" with the intent of helping them to develop new skills. This is also a good way to guide and evaluate a person for an advanced opportunity, before telling them what you have in mind and making a verbal commitment. If they don't demonstrate the skills or temperament needed in the "special project", you will not need to renege on a verbal commitment.

Delegate tasks that are better done by others. Be honest with yourself. Some people who report to us have talents and skills we do not necessarily have. Because they are often *closer* to a problem or opportunity, they are in a position to make better decisions than we can. These are the kinds of tasks that are ideal to be delegated and performed by others.

Delegate tasks that are not central to your role. Don't delegate tasks that are at the "core" of your job duties or responsibilities. This would include roles such as setting objectives, strategy, allocating resources, or evaluating performance and personnel decisions. Also, don't delegate tasks that are symbolic and expected to be performed by you! For example, if you traditionally give a speech at an annual company event or hand out *gifts* at a picnic, these are not the kind of tasks to delegate.

Delegate a variety of tasks including pleasant duties. Don't hoard all the enjoyable tasks to yourself and only give repetitive and boring tasks to others. If this is repeatedly done, the tasks you delegate will be performed without enthusiasm and decrease job satisfaction. Over time, it adds more stress to those who inherit these tasks and the quality of their work and decision-making will decline. The right balance is to delegate both pleasant and unpleasant tasks.

Consider that Will Rogers once said, "Even though you are on the right track... you'll get run over if you just sit there."

THE ART OF DELEGATION – PART 2

How a delegated task is carried out is as important as what types of tasks should be delegated. In the previous tip we discussed what kinds of tasks are appropriate to delegate. In this tip we will examine *how* to effectively delegate tasks to others! The more work involved up-front to establish and build a solid relationship between delegator and delegate, the greater the opportunities for success.

Discuss mutual responsibilities clearly. The lack of performing this first step is where the seeds of failure are planted in many delegated duties. It is essential that the delegator is specific in outlining the responsibilities expected from the delegate. Begin by outlining the objectives and ultimate goal of these new tasks. Provide your expectations including any deadlines, reports, and the level of communication you desire.

Also, discuss what your level of commitment will be in the process! What kind of resources will you provide to the delegate? Will you make sure that necessary funds are made available? Provide an overview of the amount of authority and discretion you are granting to the delegate. What kinds of decisions can be made without your approval? Can the delegate make any agreements or negotiate freely with other parties? Explain how often you will make yourself available for questions and progress reviews. The more detail and clarity that is provided at this point, the higher the chance of achieving a beneficial relationship, and avoiding confusion.

At the conclusion of your discussion make sure you both mutually "buy-in" to the commitments given by both delegator and delegate. If one or the other has doubts about another's role, this is the time to talk openly, candidly and promise your acceptance of the new roles. Don't end the meeting without both of you expressing comfort and satisfaction with this new relationship and mutual duties.

Get involved and build a pathway for success. It is important to immediately inform other co-workers about the delegate and their new role. The delegate will need the cooperation and assistance of other people to be productive. The delegator is the one who should inform others of this change in tasks and seek the support of others for the delegate. Let others know the delegate has your support and needed authority to perform their new tasks. Keep in mind that the people who need to know this may go beyond your own department or organization. It may also include suppliers and customers!

Monitor how well the delegate is doing in a moderate and balanced way. Early on, you will want to provide some oversight, but without constant monitoring or interference. Provide feedback when helpful and let the delegate know they are free to ask you for advice at any time. If you see problems or confusion at this point, it is better to respond as soon as possible before poor habits or a misunderstanding becomes entrenched. If the delegate asks you to help them with a problem, make yourself available as a mentor and coach. To develop their problem solving skills, ask them to suggest a solution to the problem.

It is strongly recommended that you do *not* become guilty of *reverse delegation,* reasserting control over a task you previously delegated! Doing this will undermine the authority and confidence of the delegate. Provide emotional and skill support to a delegate that appears to be frustrated or discouraged. Mistakes will certainly be made, but rather than being harsh or critical, allow them to become learning experiences. Discuss *why* the mistake was made and identify how similar mistakes can be avoided in the future.

Consider that William P. Steven once said, "You cannot define talent. All you can do is build the greenhouse and see if it grows."

ENCOURAGE FLEXIBILITY AND INNOVATION

In our fast paced world, change is increasing at an ever alarming rate. Within the business world the ability to be flexible to changing conditions and innovation is a matter of survival! Competition is more intense, products become obsolete sooner, customers demand greater levels of service, and there is less time to develop new products. Organizations determined to survive must be committed to acquiring newer levels of knowledge either by imitating the best practices of others or self-discovery. Organizations that learn rapidly and use newly gained knowledge to become more effective are called *learning organizations*. These firms dedicate resources to promote learning at all levels.

What are some of the ways an organization's culture can be changed to promote learning? A major emphasis should be placed on encouraging flexibility and innovation. Here are some ways to encourage these two valuable qualities...

Show an appreciation for flexibility and innovation. People who have confidence and pride in their ability to adapt and learn will be more open to change. Confident workers view change not as a burden but as an exciting new challenge. Encourage an environment where everyone views existing methods and practices as temporary...open to improvement and growth. Applaud those who examine each activity to determine if it is still needed or how it can be improved.

Promote a "systems thinking" approach. We all tend to use simplistic mental models to approach problems or opportunities. This narrow approach often leads to more problems and a limited understanding of real events. Systems thinking acknowledges complex inter-relationships and cycles. By using systems thinking, it is realized that problems have multiple causes. Actions are recognized to have multiple outcomes and perhaps some unintended side effects. Some decisions that appear to offer quick results may actually be harmful in the long run. Systems thinking accepts that a change in one part of the organization or department often elicits a response from other parts that will seek to maintain equilibrium or the status quo.

The reaction from one part or department can actually dampen the effects of the initial change! Promoting a systems thinking approach results in a more effective and realistic analysis of the true cause of problems and possible solutions.

Welcome learning opportunities from surprises and failures. It is remarkable to consider that surprises and failures can often provide greater opportunity for learning than expected outcomes and events. Expected outcomes simply confirm existing assumptions and therefore provide no new insights or fresh perspectives. Most people ignore new information or knowledge that doesn't fit into their assumptions of how things work. Point out that some of the greatest human discoveries are the results of anomalies or accidents! Demonstrate to others that surprises and failures can provide new perceptions and a chance for greater self-discovery and analysis.

Gain knowledge from outsiders. Leaders are humble enough to accept the fact that they don't know everything and can learn much from others. Some organizations and people have an ignorant and arrogant attitude toward ideas that were "not invented here." A wise leader counteracts this attitude by identifying the best practices of other organizations. First, evaluate the relevance of their practices before adopting them. Secondly, realize that imitation of others provides little competitive advantage. It is better to improve upon the best practices of other organizations by inventing new approaches not yet discovered or used.

Consider that it was Edmund Burke, who once said, "You can never plan the future by the past."

BEING AN EFFECTIVE AGENT OF CHANGE

Look into any book on business, management or leadership and you will find the vital topic of "change" considered an essential subject. The ability of individuals and organizations to change is crucial to growth, health, and survival. Leaders are often called upon to be "agents" of the change process. Visionary leadership identifies the need for positive change, charts the course of direction and leads the way down the path. If this is the case, why does almost every consultant, business scholar and manager openly admit that most attempts to produce real change completely fail? Why is there almost universal agreement that most attempts to produce lasting change result in frustration and massive resistance? Here are a few things to keep in mind;

1. *The overwhelming majority of people naturally and fervently resist change either in their personal lives or in the workplace.* We like our "comfort zone." Always doing the same things and acting the same way provides a sense of security and stability. In contrast, the process of change is viewed by most as risky and unsettling. It is viewed as an entrance to a new world of unknown outcomes. This is a pervasive environment that all leaders must accept and learn to deal with effectively.

2. *The first big mistake most leaders make when attempting to introduce change is they fail to get the valuable input of others before they introduce or begin the change process.* Too many leaders believe they single-handedly can initiate or force change upon others without ample explanation or consensus. This will guarantee greater resistance and resentment toward change even when introduced with the best of ideas or intentions. What is your reaction when change is forced upon you? How do you respond when change is thrust upon you without your opinion being considered important? If you want individuals to "buy-in" to an idea or process, it is wise to solicit their ideas and input very early in the change process.

3. *The second biggest mistake most leaders make is that they do not spend enough time inspiring and convincing everyone of the absolute need for change.* People need to be logically and emotionally inspired to change themselves or their organization.

Look at your own life. If you see a personal need for change due to observation or criticism, how successful will you be if you have not deeply convinced yourself of the need for improvement? The answer to this question can be seen in the millions of broken "resolutions" we make to ourselves during the course of a year. This is where your leadership skills will be tested and challenged. It is absolutely essential that you spend a tremendous amount of time vigorously teaching, proclaiming and convincing others why the change is necessary and healthy. Pontificating in a meeting doesn't do it. Sending a memo doesn't do it. A company wide meeting flashing a few PowerPoint slides doesn't do it. Intimidating others doesn't do it. What does do it is engaging in enthusiastic discussion with others as to why they will be better off contributing to the change process. Everyone wants a better work environment, encouragement, greater personal fulfillment, possible career advancement and potential gains in income. How and why will the change you seek to introduce contribute to their needs? If you have not prepared a convincing answer, prepare for massive amounts of resistance and frustration. People can accept the need for sacrifice and change if they are convinced it is a worthwhile process and will result in a better future.

4. *Finally, remember that as a leader you are also a promoter!* You must personally model the new change and sincerely listen to others. Show everyone you are open-minded and concerned about any new problems or challenges that arise. Others are watching you to see if you believe what you are promoting or if you are simply going through the motions. You need credibility to be an effective change agent!

Years ago, an automotive television commercial stressed the importance of routine vehicle maintenance. The slogan announced, "Pay now...or pay later." The point of the commercial was that routine maintenance is inexpensive, but the failure of a vital part is very expensive. As a leader, you can make a personal investment up-front, before the change process is introduced, or you can make a larger investment later on with greater odds of failure. The choice is yours!

Consider that is was former British Prime Minister Harold Wilson, who said, "He who rejects change is the architect of decay. The only human institution which rejects progress is the cemetery."

BE A TEAM-BUILDER

Within our modern business environment more and more work is now performed by teams rather than solely by individuals. This certainly makes sense since the complexity and speed of change of our modern world places greater performance demands on organizations. A good team brings a greater variety of skills and experiences to solve difficult problems as opposed to just one person, no matter how gifted that person is. Leaders must become team-builders to gain the greatest potential and superior accomplishment from their teams.

However, the other side of the coin reveals that building a solid team is more difficult than in the past due to greater diversity in the workplace. More than ever, workers with broad ethnic, religious and culturally diverse backgrounds work side by side as co-workers. How can a leader become a team-builder? Here are a few tips.

1. *Encourage appreciation and tolerance for diversity.* If this is not done, the group's diversity can become a source of conflict instead of strength. As a leader, foster a respect for individual differences and demonstrate the benefits of having a diverse team! Discourage the use of stereotypes used to describe group members and directly challenge individuals who make prejudiced comments. By your own example, promote an appreciation of different cultures and their unique contributions.

2. *Emphasize common values and interests.* Rather than focusing on differences, emphasize mutual interests. Identify the group's shared objectives and passionately explain why cooperation is necessary to achieve them. Help the team to understand that shared objectives are more important than self-centeredness or personal agendas. Express how it is often necessary to submerge one's personal interest to achieve great things and to reach the team's ultimate potential.

3. *Develop your own special ceremonies and symbols to identify the group's uniqueness.* Perform special actions and rituals to make group membership appear to be very special.

These are most effective when they emphasize the group's values and new traditions. Initiate ceremonies to celebrate special events, anniversaries, achievements and the addition or departure of team members. Symbols also develop a feeling of pride within the group. It may be a group name, innovative emblem, slogan or team logo. These can create a special identity for the team and unity is strengthened when members wear or display their symbols of membership.

4. *Facilitate and promote social interaction outside of work.* Your team will be more cohesive if the members get to know each other on a personal social basis. As the leader, schedule social activities such as parties, lunches, sports events or cultural activities together. It is amazing how differences fade away when people socialize together and realize their common human interests. Make sure you personally make each member feel wanted, comfortable and appreciated during these social events.

5. *Keep everyone informed about activities and achievements.* The quickest way to alienate team members is to provide little information about the achievement, plans or activities of the group. It is natural to feel unappreciated when you are left "out of the loop." Keep everyone informed about all the various activities with a personal call or memo to everyone. Remember to let each individual know how their personal effort contributes to the success of the entire team's mission!

Consider that it was President George W. Bush who said, "A leader is only as good as his team."

WHAT IS YOUR MORAL LEADERSHIP STYLE?

There is much discussion in the news today about ethics, particularly in the business sector. Many major corporations have been guilty of accounting irregularities and fraud. Each individual possesses his or her own values and ethics that are reflected in their leadership style. This is true of business executives and others in high-level management positions. This tip will discuss four particular leadership styles. Each style is built on a different level of ethical standards and can be observed along a continuum from least ethical to most ethical.

1. *The Manipulator*—the "ends justifies the means" approach
Least Ethical

This style is amoral and is driven by the motive of power and control. It is essentially an economic or egotistical ethic. The end result of any decision or action "justifies the means" taken to manipulate others. It is based on a Machiavellian ethic that views leadership unscrupulously. It is based on short-term gain and relationships which lack trust. The motives of this style are amoral but the effect upon others is typically immoral. Other stakeholders are considered unimportant and mere pawns for personal advancement.

2. *The Bureaucratic Administrator*—the "rules" approach
More Ethical

This rule-based style is founded on the rigid principles established within the organizational bureaucracy. The administrator is interested only in maintaining efficiency rather than effectiveness, by enforcing fixed rules and applying the "chain-of-command" control structure. The problem with this style is that legitimate human needs may be neglected because the ability to intercede was not included or spelled out in the rules. This creates a "sin of omission" where others are hurt unintentionally because their unique need is not included in the rigid rule-based organizational structure.

3. *The Professional Manager*—the "social contract" approach
More Ethical

This style reflects the proverbial "company man or woman,"

but with more flexibility than the bureaucratic administrator. The *professional manager's* style is based upon the organization's "social contract" between the managers and corporate executives. This agreement includes the explicit or implicit set of ethics and ground rules that govern the manager's behavior. Like the previous two management styles, the *professional manager* relies on amoral techniques and basic assumptions on how to get work done. The major ethical problem with this style is that the corporate culture may be amoral or immoral, and this will dominate the professional manager's approach due to the social contract. The collective corporate culture may lead itself astray due to Groupthink or other factors. I will provide some tips for Groupthink in the next chapter.

4. *The Transforming Leader*—the "personal ethic" approach
Most Ethical

This style is grounded on a personal ethic. This type of leader elevates the values and motives of others and is not hesitant to counter the "social contract" if it is deemed amoral or immoral. *Transforming leaders* base their effectiveness on relationships, and they actively motivate others to reach personal growth and self-actualization. They maintain a moral approach to the work environment, and in the words of William Hitt, "it raises the level of human conduct and aspirations of both leaders and led, and thus has a transforming effect on both."

Take some time to consider these four particular leadership styles. What are the ethical standards reflected in your leadership style?

Consider that it was Theodore Roosevelt who said, "No man is justified in doing evil on the ground of expediency."

MOTIVATING BEYOND MONEY

We are all aware of the fact that people are motivated by money. Virtually all workers exchange their time and talents for financial remuneration to meet their personal needs. For this reason money is indeed a powerful motivator! A wise leader knows that individuals should receive occasional *increases* in compensation to maintain a high level of motivation. However, increasing the money paid to a worker is actually a short term motivator. In time, the increase in income simply becomes the expected norm. Other individuals will appreciate a raise in salary, but may not be personally motivated by this action. It is important to learn to provide *other* forms of motivation beyond money. Here are some other forms of motivation to consider.

1. *Praise good workers in front of their peers!* Virtually everyone welcomes praise and a feeling of appreciation for what they do. Many leaders make the mistake of only praising good performance privately. The most effective form of praise is by public proclamation. Praising the high achievement of others publicly is a great way to motivate beyond money. Some leaders are simply not very good at publicly giving praise. If you have a difficulty doing this in front of others, then do it in a general memo! Or find a key member of your team who has a natural gift of publicly offering praise and have them do it on your behalf. But, don't overuse this powerful motivator or it will lose its effectiveness.

2. *Give them special assignments.* This tip requires some time but it is highly motivating. Take the time to find out some of the special interests your workers have. Match their special interest with needed projects or special assignments! The goal is to provide them an opportunity to work at something they intensely love or enjoy doing. Make sure you tell them they have been chosen to serve this special role because you deeply appreciate and recognize their exceptional performance.

3. *Give them the ability to create their own flexible schedules.* If they work in a structured office environment, allow them to adjust their personal needs with the daily work schedule. Perhaps they visit a health club in the morning and would

appreciate coming in 30 minutes later on certain days. Perhaps they have children in a daycare center and would appreciate leaving a few minutes early on some days of the week. It may be important for them to avoid a certain traffic pattern by leaving or arriving differently than "official" workplace hours. Also, don't forget the powerful motivator of occasionally giving a good worker an afternoon off, or an entire day off *beyond* the official vacation policy.

4. *Look for advancement opportunities for good workers.* Not everyone desires a promotion in title or added responsibility, but many do. If it is not offered in a reasonable amount of time, those who are motivated by advancement opportunities will eventually feel unappreciated. If you don't have any prospects in your own department, look for advancement opportunities in other areas of the organization. Yes, you may personally lose a good worker this way, but it will be offset by the goodwill and respect you will earn throughout the organization. You will show others that you care about the interest and future of others!

5. *Simple pleasures are the best.* Don't forget that simple gestures of kindness mean a lot. Is your hardworking associate a sports fan? Get them a couple of tickets to a professional sporting event. Do they enjoy a fine meal? How about a gratis dinner at a fine restaurant for both them and their spouse? Use your imagination and you can find many ways to show appreciation and motivate good performance beyond money. Like the previous tip on special assignments (#2), it is important to take the time to discover their personal interests.

Consider that it was James Barrie who said, "Nothing is really work unless you would rather be doing something else."

LEADERSHIP AND CHARISMA

For decades it was incorrectly believed by many people that all great leaders possessed a trait called charisma. This influential trait is defined as "those who arouse fervent popular devotion and enthusiasm." It typically includes a strong personal magnetism or charm. Unfortunately, far too many people have actually defined leadership as if it was *synonymous* with charisma! Many military generals, business mavericks and coaches of athletes have been quoted extensively to promote a "winning is everything" approach to achievement or problem solving. No doubt that talented individuals like Vince Lombardi and General George S. Patton had charisma and some valuable leadership skills. It is true that when used effectively charisma can be a powerful motivating tool by those leaders who possess it. But this does not prove an exclusive link between leadership and charisma. In actuality, the majority of leaders who have ever existed or exist today do not have charisma. The reason is because it is not essential for leadership.

Sadly, some individuals who have the gift of charisma have misused this tool to manipulate and deceive followers to achieve personal gain or power. This has been a common problem throughout human history. Recent news reports about political and business corruption highlights how certain individuals have misused their power of persuasion to abuse others for selfish personal gain.

As a society, our focus should not be on those who have charisma but rather on those who lead with integrity. Author Jim Collins comments in his book *Good To Great: Why Some Companies Make the Leap...and Others Don't* (HarperCollins) that the difference between a good leader and a bad one is "the inner landscape of the leader." He spent five years studying business leaders who took their companies from good to great by maintaining outstanding performance for at least fifteen years. His conclusion is that the good leaders were "ambitious first and foremost for their cause, for the company, for the work. Not for themselves. They are self-confident, not self-centered."

Did Collins find that charisma was an essential or even

important trait for a good leader? To the contrary, he found that these leaders were "self-effacing, quiet, reserved, even shy —these leaders are a paradoxical blend of personality, humility and professional will. They are more like Lincoln and Socrates than Patton or Caesar." It is a common cultural flaw to expect leaders to exhibit charisma or to closely link leadership with charisma. This flaw has led many down a path of frustration and disillusionment when the personal charisma of a leader proved to be self-absorbed and shallow.

Instead of charisma, our culture should focus on possessing leadership qualities like being trustworthy, genuine, honest and service-minded. These are the traits that reveal the "inner landscape of the leader" and provide a long-term motivation for others to follow.

Consider that it was Confucius who said, "Humility is the solid foundation of all the virtues."

Chapter 4

DEVELOP YOUR LEADERSHIP SKILLS

Being an excellent leader goes far beyond your personality, authority or title. Making an effort to expand your core leadership skills will give you the ability to successfully manage day-to-day decisions. The first step is to candidly examine your strengths and weaknesses.

DISCOVERING YOUR CORE COMPETENCIES

Organizations have the special capability and knowledge to perform a certain type of activity very well. It is a leader's role to discover and define exactly what this capability really is! This is what is known as a *core competency*, and this is what the company should leverage. It typically involves the blending of certain technical and application skills. Researchers Hamel and Prahalid define the core competency as "the collective learning in the organization, especially [knowing] how to coordinate diverse production skills and integrate multiple streams of technologies."

However, there is an important difference between the tangible resources of a company and its core competency. Tangible resources are depleted as they are used, whereas core competencies tend to increase when used correctly. Why is this important? Knowing and exploiting your core competencies can give you an ongoing competitive advantage if used to provide high-quality services or products that can't be quickly duplicated or copied by competitors. But this can't happen if the organization's leadership does not correctly identify and build a strategy around it's own core competencies.

Here is what truly understanding your core competencies can accomplish...

1. *Discovering this special capability can help the organization to focus on what it really does well and avoid diluting its resources on a poor strategy.*

2. *If your organization is already prosperous, it can help you to remain competitive and guide you to the right kinds of businesses in which to diversify.*

3. *If your organization is in decline, it can revitalize itself by discovering and focusing on its core competencies. This often means shedding the business of markets, products or services that are not a part of the new strategy.*

Great care must be taken not to poorly define the organization's core competencies. Here are a couple of interesting examples.

Circuit City® has a demonstrated core competency selling electronics to the retail market in its many megastores. However, in 1993 it entered the used car market and eventually opened 23 CarMax® stores in seven states. By 1998 they accepted the fact that this decision was a large mistake, as CarMax's losses were pulling down Circuit City's results. Perhaps a strategy had been built upon a misguided core competency like the "operation of super efficient megastores with sophisticated distribution systems." Whatever the reason, the core competency of Circuit City® had been defined improperly, and this was a costly error.

Starbucks® is a highly successful company roasting and selling specialty coffee to the retail market in its many convenient locations. Recently they attempted to sell prepackaged sandwiches made each morning at a central location and then sent to stores to sell throughout the day. But the attempt failed for two reasons. Starbucks® isn't structured to sell sandwiches, and customers wanted fresh sandwiches which would require additional space, storage and training. Founder Howard Schultz opined, "We recognize more than ever that our core competency is roasting and selling the best coffee in the world."

Consider that it was Eric Hoffer who wrote, "Our greatest weariness comes from work not done."

WHAT IS A LEARNING ORGANIZATION?

A new movement is slowly taking place in modern business. As it continues, it will produce the most positive and lasting change ever experienced in the workplace. What is this movement? It is the commitment to become a *learning organization*. This phrase has been coined by management experts to describe organizations dedicated to learning new things and using that knowledge to become more effective. Here is what this commitment means. Within these learning organizations all decisions are based as much on the desire to learn and gain knowledge as they are to achieve short-term performance.

What are some of the characteristics of learning organizations? There is a lot of emphasis placed on how to develop and understand why things work and how they can be refined. There is an attitude of continuous learning that supports the workplace environment. Resources are invested in people to promote learning, provide formal training programs, analyze processes and evaluate outcomes. Many leaders have recognized that it is essential to develop people at every level of the organization by promoting learning and continuous improvement. The positive nature of this environment also benefits the worker outside of the workplace in a personal way! Within a learning organization, a strategic focus is placed on discovering new knowledge and imitating the best practices of others. However, new knowledge is useless unless it is utilized! It is one thing to discover knowledge; it is another thing to use it effectively. This is where leadership can have a powerful influence.

Leaders value the learning organization concept. They understand that they have a vital role to play in nurturing the right environment. Here are some guidelines to promote a learning organization.

Demonstrate an appreciation for learning and flexibility—Every *existing* training activity in the organization should be examined to evaluate if it is still needed, or how it can be improved. If it is no longer effective it should be replaced with one that energizes the attendees. Organizational change is more acceptable to people who develop confidence and pride in their capacity to learn new things. Encourage all workers to evaluate their skills and tasks with flexibility and innovation.

Shape learning opportunities from surprises and failures —Most people tend to ignore or discount sudden information that doesn't fit their expectations or assumptions of how things work. Yet, some of the most impressive discoveries of humankind have come about by accident. Encourage others to use unexpected results to reexamine their assumptions and expectations. Endorse these opportunities as a way to learn something new and apply it.

Promote and facilitate learning by individuals—An organization can only grow when individual members of that organization are learning. As a leader, cultivate a culture that honors and respects individual learning. This includes the strong cultural values of personal development and lifelong education. Programs that provide financial assistance for outside education promote this value and reward individual workers who support it.

Encourage experimentation—Small-scale experiments provide a chance to try out new ideas without the risk involved in major change. In addition, people are also more open-minded to try new approaches on a small scale rather than completely abandoning traditional practices. Of course, how effective the experiment will be depends on how well it is designed and executed.

Acquire the "best practices" of others—Identify and adopt the best practices of successful organizations. This can be a useful source of innovation. However, be flexible enough to modify or evaluate the relevance of these practices for your particular organization. Don't simply be an imitator, but improve and invent new approaches from the best practices of others.

As we can see, leaders should take an active role in advancing the culture of continuous learning throughout the entire organization and within individuals. This is an investment in the future that will help the organization to adapt more quickly and innovatively to changing global markets.

Consider that it was Herbert Spencer, who wrote, "The great aim of education is not knowledge, but action."

ARE YOU LISTENING? – PART 1

To be successful leaders, we must develop the vital skill of active listening. This is part of an overall need for effective oral communication. *Active listening* is the ability to listen intently to what others are saying, understand what they are communicating, and show a response of positive affirmation that we are hearing and comprehending their remarks. Below are the first *six* guidelines you can use to improve your active listening skills.

Make yourself available—Obviously effective leaders cannot listen to others if they cloister themselves in their office and make themselves hard to find! This simply feeds the old hierarchal stereotype that leaders are aloof and *think* they are superior to others. Be sure to have an "open door" policy and allow others come to you without much notice. If you are busy and unavailable, immediately set an appointment with anyone who asks for your time. They should walk away from you knowing you care about their needs and possessing an appointment to see you again.

Sustain your attention—Show you value another's comments by providing *both* verbal and nonverbal signals that you are indeed listening. This includes good eye contact, verbal acknowledgement, confirming facial expressions and an alert posture. Make an effort to avoid any distractions during the conversation that will affect your ability to sustain your attention.

Don't over-interpret—Do not jump to a conclusion about what is being said. Early in a conversation, the information is usually too imprecise or incomplete to make a proper analysis of what the speaker is intending. Seek first to understand, and only afterward to be understood. Withhold any early impressions until they are validated through further communication.

Avoid being immediately judgmental—Being judgmental makes it far more difficult to really understand what the speaker is saying. It is all too common for a listener to *rapidly* decide that a message is *right* or *wrong* or the speaker is good or bad and make a judgmental remark. This only stunts the ability to communicate and typically produces defensiveness. Being judgmental provokes the listener to mentally construct a reply rather than truly listen to the speaker.

Suspend your preconceptions and biases—Don't simply assume that others have the same attitudes, motives or values as you do. Empathy means that we understand another's perceptions and feelings. However, if you harbor preconceptions or biases toward others, you can't have *proper* empathy. You will misinterpret the message of the speaker through a narrow-minded filter of your personal preconceptions. Make an active effort to learn what the other person is really trying to communicate, even if they are having difficulty expressing it.

Restate what is said—Paraphrasing what the speaker communicates is a remarkably effective skill in active listening. It confirms to the speaker that you are actively listening to what they have said. It also allows you to verbally confirm your understanding of what was said. Finally, it permits the speaker to correct any assumptions you may have of what has just been stated.

In our next tip we will discuss more ways to develop active listening skills.

Consider that it was Boris Marshalov who wrote, "Congress is so strange. A man gets up to speak and says nothing. Nobody listens—and then everybody disagrees."

ARE YOU LISTENING? – PART 2

In this tip we continue our discussion of *active* listening. We have to train ourselves to be active listeners, since it does not come naturally. Most of the time we are already preparing to *speak again,* rather than deeply listening when another speaks. In most conversations, the person who does most of the talking is the one who learns the least about the other person. If you aspire to be a respected leader, you must become a good listener. Here are *four* more guidelines to help you become an active listener.

Exhibit empathy—Most people fear ridicule or rejection when they are expressing their ideas and opinions. If the listener implies they disapprove of the person, or their feelings, it only inhibits further communication. Respond to the speaker with your manner and speech, showing you really care about what the speaker is saying and feeling. This is especially important if you don't agree with what is being said. One can disagree without being disagreeable!

Use probing remarks to overcome inhibitions—Aside from empathy, another way to draw a speaker out of their apprehensions is to ask nonthreatening questions that probe their feelings. Examples of these include, "How do you feel about that?" or "Can you remember a specific example of when that happened?" or "What happened next?" When these are done without a hint of rejection or evaluation, they can make the speaker feel more comfortable in communicating.

Promote suggestions for helping others to solve problems—Good leaders know that it is more effective to help others solve their problems rather than offering advice. Many people are sensitive about accepting advice from others. A common goal of sound leadership is to teach others to develop leadership skills by taking the initiative to deal with problems on their own. This can also be encouraged by asking some probing questions such as, "What would you recommend should be done?" or "What are the alternatives?" or "How would you accomplish that?"

Complement your interaction—Being a good communicator

means that we develop a proper sense of when to re-enter a conversation. This means we are willing to adjust our own speaking patterns to correspond with the qualities of another person. Sound communication is disrupted when both individuals attempt to talk simultaneously or interrupt each other. Other disruptions can occur when one makes comments that show a clear disregard for what was just communicated by another, or if you abruptly change topics in the middle of a conversation. Be sensitive and aware of these disruptions and adjust your interaction skills in these situations to complement the existing communication.

Consider that it was Kelly Stephens who wrote, "If you want people to notice your faults, start giving advice."

CORRECTING A CO-WORKER

One of the most difficult tasks a leader has is to establish and nurture a vision for their group or organization. Keeping all co-workers excited and moving toward the same goal can be a great challenge. This becomes even more daunting when a member of the team needs to be corrected. There may be many reasons for having a corrective discussion with a co-worker. It may be because of an attitude, an open remark, spreading an unhealthy rumor, or violating a confidence. Allowing these negative traits to continue can erode the trust and confidence of the entire team. As a leader, it will occasionally be necessary to address this delicate issue. How can a leader have a corrective discussion that has positive and constructive results? Here are some points to ponder.

1. *Correct an individual privately in an atmosphere of a "one-on-one" chat.* Only under the rarest of circumstances should you correct someone in public. Doing this almost guarantees the creation of lingering resentment or bitterness toward you and the organization. The purpose of private correction is to sincerely help the individual, and benefit the entire team by preserving the positive skills and talents of the individual.

2. *Begin the conversation with a personal and positive approach.* It is important to begin by letting the person know you appreciate their contribution and abilities. Point out a few positive qualities they possess that you admire and respect. Don't begin the conversation by launching into a diatribe about a problem or perceived weakness on their part. This will backfire and the individual will probably "return fire" by letting you know about all of your faults. Start out slowly, and begin by showing the person that you recognize their strengths and contribution. Let them know you really care about them!

3. *As you direct the conversation toward the discussion of a problem, remember to listen.* This provides you an opportunity to analyze the problem from a fresh perspective. Address the issue and allow the individual to explain it from their perspective. Again, simply "cutting them off" in mid-sentence is sure to create

resentment. Allow them to talk and express their feelings. Next, it is your turn...

4. *Begin by clearly and patiently expressing the problem, as you perceive it.* Show the negative consequences of the individual's actions and how they affect not only you but also the entire team and its mission. Explain how their actions may erode their credibility and respect from others. Tell them clearly that you expect this conduct to cease because it is counterproductive. Avoid using a tone of anger or raising your voice. Set the right example of maturity and dignity in your conduct. Remember, the goal is to point out a legitimate problem and help the individual to recognize and overcome their part in it. Offer some positive suggestions on how past experiences could have been handled!

5. *Finally, conclude the conversation by once again reminding your co-worker of how much you value their input and personal talents.* You want to end the conversation in a positive manner. You want the individual to leave the conversation clearly knowing their responsibility is to change, but also feeling like they are still appreciated and have a vital role to play within the team.

Consider that is was Walter E. Washington who said, "People are not an interruption of our business, people are our business."

COMMUNICATION SKILLS FOR A GROUP LEADER

One of the most important roles of a leader is to engage in clear and constructive communication with others. This is especially true when working with committees or groups. Leadership is a multi-faceted task that relies on strong communication skills. Here are seven communication skills for a group leader in today's complex business environment.

1. *Know how to keep a discussion general when necessary, rather than specific and personal.* Unfortunately many discussions evolve into becoming personal with accusations or even "name calling." Some individuals desire to criticize others in an effort to draw attention away from the real issues. Don't be afraid to remind the speaker that the major goal of problem solving is to analyze what is wrong, rather than who is wrong. Someone's performance, or lack of it, may be an important issue, but it should also be a *separate* issue.

2. *Know how to deal with errors in statement of fact.* It is common for people to "shoot from the hip" in an effort to support their own personal agenda or to encourage an emotional response from you. Before you react, be sure to ask where the information has come from. Ask how reliable the speaker believes it is. Gently challenge them if you feel suspicious of the validity. If you later find the information to be in error, patiently remind the speaker that factual errors can lead to poor decision making or lost opportunities. If you find that an individual routinely communicates lies or errors in a deliberate manner, it is time to sternly remind them of their ethical responsibilities.

3. *Know how to link discussion to action.* An old motto states that, "When all is said and done, much more will be said than is ever done." Many committees are notorious for recommending ideas that never turn into action. Make sure that you end meetings with action items. Give assignments to various individuals and deadlines for action items to be achieved. Discussion is a valuable asset, but it must be translated into action to achieve real results. If your task as a committee is to provide recommendations along with findings, clearly specify the actions the committee recommends.

4. *Know how to stimulate discussion among individuals who are shy or not articulate.* Certain people are not gifted in speech. This may be the result of personality, lack of esteem or fear from past negative experiences. Yet, these individuals often have much to contribute in sound ideas and comments. Make an effort to help them feel comfortable within an environment that respects and values their comments. Do not allow others to ridicule or chide them because of their lack of verbal communication skills. Allow them to write down their comments in the form of a report if they prefer. Ask open ended questions that require some explanation from them rather than a simple "yes or no" answer.

5. *Know how and when to summarize.* There comes a point in a discussion where valid and necessary information has been exchanged. Beyond this point it can simply become rehashing everything that has already been discussed. This can quickly develop into the proverbial "beating the dead horse." When you sense this occurring, it is time to summarize. Take the major ideas expressed and encapsulate them into a brief and logical outline. There comes a point in all communication when it is time to move on!

6. *Know how to control the discussion monopolizer.* Almost every group or committee has at least one individual who attempts to monopolize all discussion. When this occurs it is time to take action. Go around the room and say, "I would like everyone individually to comment on this." If the *monopolizer* interrupts, patiently ask them not to do so and go back to the person who was speaking. If the interruptions continue, use humor to get the monopolizer to see the need of allowing others to speak. If necessary, talk to them privately and ask them to respect the ability of others to also express their views. Remind them that people were given two ears and only one mouth for a good reason.

7. *Know how to deal with hecklers.* Ever have someone who can't seem to stop themselves from making offensive "wisecracks" to others or who uses sarcasm excessively to deride others? Don't accept it for long! It can have a serious influence on the morale of others. It can also be hurtful and cause positive contributors to withdraw from making comments or offering ideas. Talk to

this person privately, and plainly help them to understand you do not find this behavior to be acceptable. If this doesn't work, you may have to repeat this lecture to them in a group setting after they make another "wisecrack." Let everyone know that you have a good sense of humor, but when it comes to offending others with hurtful remarks, one has definitely crossed the line of acceptable behavior.

Consider that it was Abraham Lincoln who said, "Everyone likes a compliment."

LEADERSHIP AND EFFECTIVE VOICEMAIL

For those of us in the modern business world, voicemail is a mixed blessing that has provided both a negative and positive influence in the workplace. Sadly, many individuals now use voicemail as a way to hide behind a digital message even though they are clearly available and able to pick up the phone. Yet, in a positive way, the use of voicemail allows the caller to leave a detailed message and communicate more effectively compared to sending email or leaving a message filtered through another person. How you use voicemail leaves a distinct impression about your leadership skills and level of professionalism. Here are some tips to help you understand how to use voicemail more effectively.

When you are the caller...

The strength of voicemail is the ability to leave a detailed message in a short period of time. However, this strength is only apparent if we speak clearly and get to the point quickly. When leaving a message, immediately identify yourself and provide the time and day you are calling. Get to the heart of your message within a few sentences and if you desire a return call, ask for it. Let the person you are calling know when is a good time to call you back! Don't ramble, and remember that a forty-five second voicemail is not intended as a replacement for a needed five minute telephone conversation. If you leave a phone number, speak slowly and even repeat it if the individual you are calling does not have it. The most common complaint of people listening to a voicemail message is a caller leaving a garbled last name or phone number.

When you are recording your outgoing voicemail message...

Some people create new messages routinely or on a regular basis. Keep the following important points in mind as you create your personalized messages.

Remember your recording tells the caller a lot about yourself.

1. *Energize your message.* A monotone voice comes across as unfriendly or uninterested. Insert some energy and enthusiasm

into your words. One way to do this is to stand up and smile while you are creating your message. Believe it or not, people can hear the difference a smile can make while a person is speaking. Standing makes your voice sound richer as it comes more deeply from your chest.

2. *Minimize the "I" statements.* It is only natural to use some "I" statements like, "I am not available at this time." However, over usage of "I" statements imply you are self-centered or egotistical. If you do this, you can balance your message by replacing some of the "I" statements with "You" statements. For example, "You have reached the office of..." This shows consideration to the caller and takes the focus off of yourself.

3. *Be creative but not cute.* It is great to show some creativity or flare in your message. Perhaps you have a special greeting or farewell phrase that is your hallmark. That is fine and shows you are a risk taker. But, what may be an acceptable message at your residence may be on the edge at your place of business. In the office it is best to avoid creating a voicemail that contains the chorus to a popular song or greetings from your pet. You want to be creative and a professional!

4. *Speak slowly and clearly.* Slowly does not mean S..L.. O..W..L..Y.

On the one hand, you don't want to sound tired or like you are reading a movie script. On the other hand, if you speak too swiftly you will sound stressed or rushed. Speak in a relaxed tone that tells all callers you are calm and in control.

5. *Brevity is best.* Try to keep your message shorter than 10 seconds. A longer message may give the impression that you are inconsiderate of other people's time. When someone discovers you are not available, they just want to leave a message. They typically are not interested in why you can't come to the phone. An exception to this is when you will be away from the office for an extended period of time such as a vacation or business trip. In this case it is certainly advisable to let the caller know when you will return to the office.

Consider that Robert Frost once said, "Half the world is composed of people who have something to say and can't, and the other half who have nothing to say and keep on saying it."

LEADERSHIP IN E-MAIL MESSAGES

It is reported that well over twenty million workers worldwide are connected by e-mail networks, and that number is growing rapidly. E-mail has become a major and primary means of personal communication. Leaders know that e-mail can be an effective or destructive tool to correspond depending on how wisely it is used. Mastering this modern technology is a real advantage for those who learn how to glean the best from it, and it can dramatically increase our productivity. Here are some powerful ways a leader can effectively use e-mail communication and avoid its abuse.

Don't forget that what you communicate is in writing. Remember that e-mail can be a form of permanent communication. Because it is electronic, it can also be retrieved much more quickly and easily than mere paper generated communication. Never assume that what you write in an e-mail will not be read by others aside from the intended party. Just because you may forget about it, doesn't mean it won't surface again at a later date. Be aware of this potential and be careful what you say! Don't leave a permanent message in writing that is better said in person or on the telephone.

Watch your tone and your wording more than ever. E-mail has a way of coming across to the reader more sternly or strongly than originally intended by the sender. For example, sarcasm can be perceived as extremely offensive. Don't type all your words in capital letters or use fragmented incomplete sentences. Also, avoid words that appear to contradict your message. One example of this is usage of the word "but." If you say, "I totally agree with your thoughts, but I also feel...," it will make the reader wonder if you totally agree with them or not! In this case it is better to replace the word "but" with "and." Setting a positive tone and carefully choosing the right wording will make your communication more effective and persuasive.

Use E-mail only when appropriate to use. Some managers find e-mail communication so convenient they have forgotten to use common sense! Don't do or say things in e-mail as an excuse to hide behind your computer terminal. E-mail is not the proper forum for disciplinary actions, performance reviews or obscene joke telling. It is not a replacement for "management by walking around" or having personal contact with others. There are many things that are only suitable to carry out in person. Many other actions are only really effective when communicated one-on-one, like personally questioning an important decision.

Take your communication to the next level. Leaders know that it is usually the small things they do and say that make a big difference. It is the quick thank you card or short complementary memo that can leave a deep impression by showing you care and appreciate others. In the past, this involved a lot of time. It required the purchase of individual cards, time to handwrite a few vital words, an envelope and often a postage stamp. Because this was a multi-step process, it was seldom performed. However, with the advent of e-mail, it is now an easy one step process to send a quick note of thanks or appreciation electronically! What used to take many minutes to do can now take a few seconds! Use e-mail to expand your ways to encourage and motivate others more often.

The modern use of e-mail can make a leader's role far more productive if used properly. Take the time to learn all of the benefits and features of your e-mail software. It can make many tasks that were previously time consuming and redundant far more enjoyable and interesting.

Consider that it was Benjamin Disraeli who said, "Where we do not respect, we cease to love."

DEALING WITH THE WORKPLACE BULLY

If you have spent a considerable amount of time working in an office or at a manufacturing plant, chances are you have discovered a workplace bully! Some common bullying tactics include creating arbitrary rules to harass a worker, isolating a worker, making unreasonable demands, insulting or putting down a worker, and yelling or screaming at a worker. Other tactics include blaming others for mistakes, taking credit for another's work and casting doubt on the quality of another person's work.

Allowing bullies to roam the workplace takes a severe toll on a worker's mental and physical health. If allowed to continue, it can cause depression and post-traumatic stress disorder. Bullying adds dramatically increased costs to companies, including lost productivity, increased sick time and employee turnover. As Gary Namie, an organizational psychologist and co-author of *The Bully at Work* has said, "Take a look at the dollars these jerks cost. You don't have to be a tenderhearted fellow. If you are just a cold-blooded, cost-benefit kind of guy, you'd understand that the bully has to go."

Sadly, some research indicates that when the target confronts the bully, it is the bully who usually keeps their job. Up to seventy percent of the time the target either gets fired for exposing the bully to management or quits to escape the situation. In addition, as long as the bully does not stalk, sexually harass or physically touch the target, their actions are not considered illegal.

Some recent surveys indicate the following problems in the American workplace associated with bullying. Some of these results may surprise you!

- *Seven times out of ten the bully outranks, or has a superior title, than the target person.*

- *A female is the target in eight out of every ten cases.*

- *In six of ten cases a female is the bully! This is because they often see that aggression is rewarded in the workplace culture.*

- *About one worker in six is bullied in any given year.*

- *Thirty percent of the targets are in jobs of an equal rank or even higher rank than the bully.*

What are some of the things a leader can do to eliminate the attitude of bullying in their workplace? Here are a few things to consider...

1. *What kind of example are you and other senior managers setting?* Are you modeling the right positive culture by your own actions and demeanor? As Rick Banning, a human resource consultant in Boston has written, "The tone is set at the top. It's real tricky if the CEO's the bully."

2. *When someone comes to you with a complaint of being the target of bullying, take the time to listen and do some internal investigation.* Be a little more observant of what is going on with the individuals in question. It takes a lot of courage or desperation for someone to come to you and point out this kind of a problem! That person knows they are putting their job and future on the line to do this so don't simply dismiss the complaint. If the person is a good employee, you will most likely lose him or her if you do little or nothing. Monitor complaints to see how bad the problem really is.

3. *Examine the organizational culture.* What is in the existing culture that allows this kind of behavior to exist? Have others been rewarded or promoted who were bullies? How many excellent employees have been lost in the past few years because they were bullied? What indications have there been in the past that should have alerted you to this problem?

4. *Consider writing a policy that specifically addresses psychological harassment.* Then set up a credible enforcement process that applies to every employee at every level throughout the organization.

The key is to firmly establish, foster and enforce an environment of mutual respect among all workers at all levels! Let it be known that bullying behavior is unacceptable and will not be tolerated in the workplace culture. Encourage a series of workshops to teach managers the effective positive ways to motivate employees.

Consider that it was Samuel Butler who said, "Silence is not always tact and it is tact that is golden, not silence."

LEADERSHIP AND CONFRONTATION?

A few years ago, I had the privilege of providing a *weLEAD* leadership seminar to a group of educators at Villanova University. I was impressed by the enthusiasm and dedication that this fine group demonstrated. As I finished the second day, we opened up a "questions and answer" session to the audience. One particular educator had a dilemma. She worked with an individual supervisor who was not responsive to the leadership skills I had been teaching the past two days. Furthermore, this supervisor was using outdated skills and an ineffective approach communicating with others. She asked, "What can I do?" She did not appear to accept my answer. I suggested she patiently and tactfully sit down with the supervisor and *express* her concerns. I encouraged her to gently tell the individual that his approach is hurting others and is not very effective. I also encouraged her to begin the conversation by telling her supervisor how much his good skills and fine qualities are appreciated. As I concluded my answer, you could see the look of resignation on her face. Her expression said, "Oh, no I just *can't* do that!"

Being a leader is not easy, and it often requires the ability to take risks and even confront individuals who are harming others or themselves. One should not take the need to confront an individual or situation lightly. It is a highly emotional event, and we naturally feel apprehensive. It requires good planning, the right environment and the genuine intention to help someone to see themself or their actions as others see them. Be prepared to discuss factual events and real life examples, not simply hearsay or rumor. It is easy to procrastinate or hope that if we wait long enough perhaps the problem will go away. Sadly, the problem seldom does, and meanwhile serious damage can be done to the group or organization. If handled with the *proper* attitude and approach, a confrontation can usually become simply an unpleasant event rather than a heated or angry exchange.

Peter Block comments in his book *Stewardship, Choosing Service Over Self-Interest,* "Sometimes in the spirit of participation, managers pull back too far. If we confront dysfunctional behavior, we get accused of being insincere in our efforts to give up control. We are told we are not walking our talk. Don't buy it. There is tyranny in the claim that we cannot confront people or even express anger when we are partners."

Please remember that leaders seek positive change, and this is done through our *influence*. If we have taken the time to build relationships with others, when we are compelled to confront them, they will be more receptive.

Consider that it was Abraham Lincoln who wrote the following quote regarding leadership, "It often requires more courage to dare to do right than to fear to do wrong."

WHAT CO-WORKERS REALLY WANT MOST

An interesting anomaly has occurred in recent surveys taken in the workplace. When CEO's, Vice Presidents or other senior managers are asked what they *think* employees want most to be content, they typically answer more money, prestige, advancement, an impressive title, or increased responsibility. However, when employees are asked the same question, these "wants" are typically not at the top of the list! What employees and co-workers say they really want most is to be appreciated! Perhaps you have heard the old business commentary about how unappreciated many workers feel. The worker remarks, "doing something good and productive around here is like loosing control of your bladder while wearing a dark suit. You get a warm feeling inside, but nobody seems to notice!"

Indeed, surveys reveal a large *gap* between what senior level managers believe co-workers want and what *they* say they really want! In today's workplace, any manager who fails to show genuine thankfulness for the work, commitment and dedication of co-workers will be perceived as selfish and insensitive.

It seems so simple and obvious, yet there is a tremendous need for greater appreciation to be shown in the workplace. Why does this problem exist? There are a number of complex reasons. Traditionally the role of managers was seen as a way to control workers. Many managers had a paternalistic attitude toward others and it was thought that showing little appreciation was a way to keep a distance from them and show who was "in charge." Some feared that complimenting workers or thanking them for an outstanding effort would encourage them to ask for more money. Far too many managers desired to be feared rather than respected, and used intimidation as an attempt to motivate workers. Since intimidation and fear was their modus operandi, there was little room to express appreciation.

So how can you fulfill the real need of coworkers and associates by showing genuine gratitude? I will briefly discuss *two* valuable ways...

1. *Make a concerted effort to verbally tell fellow workers how*

much they contribute to the overall success of the organization. All employees have strengths as well as weaknesses. Focus on their strengths and use every opportunity possible to express thankfulness for their skills and efforts. Do this even if they are not perfect or do not perform tasks exactly the way you would have performed them. As Ken Blanchard proclaimed in his classic book entitled *The One Minute Manager*, catch others doing something right! Let them know you noticed and are grateful!

2. *Remember, it is not enough to simply "tell" coworkers how appreciated they are!* You must also show them with actions. In this case, little things do mean a lot. Give occasional small gifts, bring in bakery items as a snack, offer some unexpected time off, and praise them in a meeting or in a memo. Use your imagination depending on your workplace but remember to regularly show your appreciation to others. Be *specific* when expressing your appreciation, as using vague flattery or generic slogans may come across to others as forced and insincere.

Finally, there is one other side benefit of showing routine appreciation to others. When a time arrives that you must correct a coworker or point out a problem, you will have more credibility if you have a reputation of being a caring and sensitive individual. However, if you are only known and recognized as an unappreciative critic you are likely to create bitterness and lasting resentment when you do point out a problem or weakness to others. Remember that people don't care how much you know until they know how much you care.

Consider that is was Dr. J. Howard Baker who wrote, "Effective leaders are obsessed with finding something good about an employee. They are very alert to opportunities to celebrate the achievement of others."

AFTER THE BIG DECISION IS MADE...

It's finally happened! After a series of meetings and hours of collaboration a big decision has been made. It was an important event, and it took a tremendous amount of resources and energy to come to the right conclusion. What are the next few essential things a leader must do? Many leaders have failed to use the proper skills to *implement* an important decision and have been shocked to see it flounder! Leadership does not end when a decision is made. The next few important steps help to achieve closure and ensure the decision is truly implemented. Here are *three* valuable points to consider.

1. Forward a summary of all the decisions made during the meeting.

Send a memo to everyone involved outlining what was decided at the meeting and what agreements were reached. You do not want individuals leaving the meeting who are misinterpreting the results or conclusion. You also don't want anyone to forget what was settled or ignore any assignments which were given. Your short written summary should include the meeting date, time, decisions made and results expected. This is also a good time to announce the time and location for a follow-up meeting. This puts everyone on notice that action should not be delayed until the last minute.

2. Assign and clarify everyone's responsibilities to implement the decision.

Preferably, this should be done during the meeting. However, if it was not, it is important that a crucial "action plan" is formalized and individuals assigned certain responsibilities. If this is not done, most followers will assume it is someone else's responsibility to complete important tasks. Secondly, a number of individuals may collide while working on the same task. You don't want group members duplicating the very same efforts or tasks. The decision(s) made are too important to be ambiguous or confusing.

3. Conduct a follow-up meeting to survey progress.

Many good group decisions have become unsuccessful

because no one followed through with the original conclusion. When a leader schedules a meeting and personally conducts it, there is a strong degree of importance and immediacy assigned within the minds of the followers. This becomes a priority and individuals make an extra effort to come to the meeting prepared to show they are keeping their responsibilities! This is the time to ask questions, probe for any obstacles that have been encountered and encourage others on what has been accomplished.

These simple steps can help a good decision become a reality. Leadership is a process that must be exercised from beginning to end.

Consider that it was Benjamin Franklin who wrote, "The busy man has few idle visitors; to the boiling pot the flies come not."

TIPS FOR "BRAINSTORMING"

There are often times when a leader is looking for a "breakthrough" to solve a serious problem or to help the organization to reach a higher level of achievement. These are situations where *brainstorming* may be helpful! Brainstorming is a procedure that encourages group members to verbally offer any spontaneous ideas that immediately come to mind. These ideas are written on a blackboard or easel and no negative comments or gestures are allowed. Other members of the group are encouraged to build and expand upon the ideas. Brainstorming is considered helpful in stimulating creativity and reducing inhibition in problem solving. It also reduces the domination of the group by certain aggressive individuals since contributions are expected to be brief and spontaneous.

The key to successful brainstorming is the ability of the leader to take a moderator's role and eliminate the natural inhibitions people have about offering their personal ideas without ridicule or judgment. Those who participate in brainstorming sessions allow themselves to become vulnerable and the leader must do everything possible to insure that others do not take advantage of this vulnerability. As a leader, absolutely allow no criticism of ideas during a brainstorming session! Here are some other tips that can promote a successful brainstorming meeting...

Send a short briefing to the attendees before the meeting begins. It is a good idea to have members of the group pondering the concept or purpose of the meeting before they begin the session. Spontaneous ideas are good, but they are also enhanced when one has had some time to think about a concept or problem in advance.

Small groups are better than large ones. Try to keep the group smaller than ten in number. Remember that people become more inhibited, and feel greater vulnerability, in larger groups of people. Smaller groups also have a higher energy level, are more cohesive and permit ideas to easily feed off each other.

Conduct the meetings in the morning. People are fresher and more creative in the morning and mid-morning hours. Near the end of the day, people become mentally tired and begin thinking about non-work activities.

Invite the "unexpected" to attend the meeting! Think of someone who can bring a novel or fresh perspective to the meeting. Perhaps you can invite a new employee, or a secretary, or an accountant or the janitor. The purpose of a brainstorming session is to bring to the surface completely new and refreshing thoughts or concepts from people who look at opportunities or problems differently than we normally do. There are serious problems that can occur from Groupthink and I encourage you carefully review the upcoming tip on this subject.

Consider that it was John Le Carre who said, "The desk is a dangerous place from which to watch the world."

STOP ANALYSIS PARALYSIS

Perhaps one major quality that defines leadership is the ability to get things done. A leader understands that mere activity isn't real achievement. Attaining the *right results* is achievement! Many leaders have the fatal problem of *analysis paralysis*. It is often demonstrated by constant requests for more statistics, reports, studies, evaluations and meetings. This process is usually accompanied by little real decision-making because more "study" or "research" always needs to be done! The myth involved with an *analysis paralysis* mindset is that mere activity is equated with achievement.

It is certainly true that leaders must search for valid information to make sound judgements. It is also true that effective leadership uses various analytical skills to sort facts from assumptions in the decision-making process. Yes, wise leaders do establish and monitor valuable processes to analyze important feedback on the results of past decisions and actions. The difference is that analysis paralysis causes people to struggle to get *beyond* proposals, systems, reports and meetings to really accomplish anything substantial. This may be due to many reasons, including the fear of failure among the management team members. Many years ago I worked for a small family-owned business that struggled seriously with this problem. Day after day was filled with meetings, more talk, analysis, surveys, strategy sessions, and finally inaction. One of the family members had a plaque in his office that aptly read, "When all is said and done...much more will be said than is ever done!" Many consultants look back after the demise of organizations and realize that failure was often accelerated not by the decisions that were made, but by the decisions it failed to make at critical times.

Here are some ways to *guard* against analysis paralysis...

1. *Set deadlines on projects and major decisions.* Everyone in the organization should understand that a time limitation exists for the decision-making process of a project. Only during rare situations should the deadline be extended. These situations would include a sudden change in market or competitive

environments that may legitimately be cause for reevaluation. If potential decisions are allowed to be open-ended without an established deadline, odds are that the tough decisions will be avoided!

2. *Evaluate the locus of control of your entire management team.* You may be in for a shock, and it may provide an answer to a large part of the problem of analysis paralysis. Your *locus of control* is a trait measured by a personality scale originally developed by Julian Rotter. Most individuals have a tendency to have either a strong *internal* locus of control orientation or strong *external* locus of control orientation. Those with a strong internal locus of control believe most events that occur in their lives are determined by their own actions rather than by chance. In contrast, those with a strong external locus of control believe most events occur by chance or circumstance and conclude they have little control over fate, or to change their lives. Those with an internal orientation tend to accept more responsibility for their actions and for organizational performance. Research indicates that those with a strong internal locus of control are also more flexible, innovative, adaptive and take more initiative in solving problems. What is your locus of control orientation? Perhaps a large part of your management team have an external locus of control. Or, perhaps they are simply following your example!

3. *If you believe you have a problem, compensate by getting help.* Effective leaders acknowledge they have weaknesses and learn to rely on competent associates or peers who have the strengths they lack. Ask this associate to *confidentially* come to you and alert you to the tendency of analysis paralysis when it becomes evident to them. Part of the solution to this problem is recognizing the weakness in yourself or your team and taking the necessary steps to modify or change behavior.

Consider that it was General George C. Marshall who said, "Don't fight the problem; decide it."

BEWARE OF GROUPTHINK

O ften times when I am driving a car I look ahead and view into the back window of the vehicle ahead of me. Sometimes I see a small statue or figure looking out the rear window back at me. It is typically a small bobble head statue of an animal, athlete or entertainer. The head of the statue is attached to a spring and because of road vibration the head of the figure is constantly nodding up and down. It reminds me of a serious leadership problem called "groupthink"!

Groupthink is the tendency of decision-makers to join together around a policy or person without questioning basic assumptions. An emotional bond of conformity can cause the group to filter out rational information that may question a policy or decision. Groupthink can also cause a group of decision-makers to rationalize a poor decision after-the-fact. Many poor decisions and faulty strategic plans are a result of groupthink. Whereas discord and conflict among individuals are *one* major pitfall among decision-makers, groupthink is a major pitfall on the *other side* of the pendulum. Group cohesiveness is a good quality and something we should all strive for, but groupthink takes this cohesiveness to the extreme.

Groupthink can happen in any environment, but it often happens following a period of success. The decision-makers become comfortable with each other and self-congratulatory. Since recent success has been achieved, they falsely assume two things. First, they tend to think they are primarily responsible for success, when in actual fact it is those who implemented and managed the changes who deserve most of the credit. Secondly, since the group bonds emotionally, they think their decisions are naturally best when in reality they have become arrogant and self-serving. This leads the group to ignore or filter out any facts or information that doesn't fit into their basic assumptions. Anyone who questions their assumptions or decisions is not considered a "team player." Finally, when their poor decisions begin to have negative consequences due to groupthink, they go on a crusade to blame others. Here is what Gary Yukl warns about groupthink in his book, *Leadership In Organizations*:

"Members develop an illusion of invulnerability, which is supported by an unfavorable view of outsiders. Critics, opponents and competitors are ridiculed and not given serious consideration. As a result the group is likely to overestimate the probability of success for a risky course of action."

So how can your organization guard against groupthink? Here are a few important steps.

1. *As a leader, encourage alternative comments.* If ideas or comments that are contrary to established basic assumptions are being cut off by others, it is time to intervene. Ask the individual to finish their comments. Remind everyone that open and frank communication is essential to good decision making.

2. *Encourage the use of committees or a task force to evaluate ideas or basic assumptions.* Don't forget those in the organization who were actually asked to implement and manage past decisions! They are a *wealth* of information and real world experience because they are closer to the front line of daily issues. Ask them to report their ideas and comments to the decision making group without fear of reprisal or intimidation. As a leader, insist that the open and honest sharing of ideas is an essential part of a healthy culture.

3. *Appoint one of the group members to play the "devil's advocate."* To avoid groupthink, postpone a decision for a few days. Ask the group to prepare a formal presentation including their data, assumptions and conclusions. Prior to the meeting, ask one of the group's most capable members to be the devil's advocate and challenge the formal presentation by looking for flaws in logic, basic assumptions, false inferences and overlooked information. Allow the devil's advocate to present a formal critique. Finally, allow the group to evaluate the results and revise the decision if necessary. It is better and easier to make changes at this stage rather than clean up the debris a poor decision will leave behind later.

4. *Maintain the right perspective as a leader.* Old-fashioned humility is a major ingredient in effective leadership. No individual or group is infallible. Make a habit of what some call "managing by walking around." Get out of your cocoon and

ask questions of those who have been affected by the group's decisions. Occasionally pick up the phone, call a customer, and get a reality check! Encouraging feedback on the results of previous decisions, including what worked and what didn't, will also help keep your feet on the *ground*. Realize that with rapidly changing technologies and cultures, many basic assumptions are in need of regular evaluation. Don't be afraid to bring in a consultant if you feel your organization or group is losing its grip on the ability to make sound decisions.

Consider that it was American author Mark Twain who humbly stated, "Between me and God we have all knowledge. God knows all there is to know, and I know the rest."

LEADING "GENERATION X" WORKERS

An important part of our modern workforce is commonly called Generation X or "Gen X" employees. These workers, who were born from the early 1960's to the late 1970's, grew up in a unique culture, and like every generation, they have their own distinct characteristics and needs. There are now more than forty million Gen X workers in the American workplace! Unfortunately, many individuals have criticized these workers as hard to motivate and lacking commitment. This type of stereotyping is unfair and dangerous. Leaders know that every generation of workers have positive and distinctive traits acquired from the culture in which they were raised. Below are *four* ways a leader can appreciate the special talents of Gen X workers and motivate them to work more effectively.

Provide access to different types of information. Remember, these workers grew up in the computer age. Unlike older workers, they quickly adopt and embrace newer ways to gain and process information. They are very skillful at analyzing different technologies and data. This allows them to solve problems by bringing together seemingly unrelated pieces of information. A leader would do best to share as much information as possible with Gen X workers instead of attempting to horde it. In the past, authoritarian managers wrongly believed that information was the source of their "power", and they did everything possible to limit it.

Allow them responsibility for various projects. Unlike Baby Boomers, Gen X workers have *more* of an independent spirit. A leader can either choose to view this from a negative perspective or treat it as an asset. Don't be obsessed with expecting them to do everything by established procedures or tradition. Give them the freedom to solve problems and find solutions in their own way within a reasonable set of guidelines. You will find that they thrive and grow in this free-thinking environment.

Give them a lot of informal feedback. Traditionally, feedback is given to workers in a formal annual performance review. Many older workers accept this workplace ritual because it meets their expectations. However, younger workers expect a great deal more feedback from managers. Gen X workers like to accomplish things in an exciting and rapid paced environment. Frequent informal feedback best suits their needs and helps to stimulate their desire to grow and become more productive.

Encourage them to "train for another job." Gen X workers know they will have many different jobs in their lifetime. They realize the old "employment contract" of previous generations no longer exists. They don't expect to stay with one company for their entire career. If you want to keep them, you will need to offer Gen X workers a variety of opportunities to develop different skills. Yes, this will make them more marketable later on, but it will also give them an incentive to stick around longer and contribute in greater ways to the organization.

Consider that it was Franklin D. Roosevelt who said, "There is a mysterious cycle in human events. To some generations much is given. Of other generations much is expected."

LEADING "PART-TIME" WORKERS

It is often difficult to lead part-time workers. Most organizations give them lower-level work, and they are often made to feel like *outsiders* by full-time employees. In addition, part-time workers are usually given a limited opportunity for advancement within the organization. This leads to a motivation problem and lower productivity. Within this negative environment, it is often difficult to "spot" the positive potential in some of these workers that may result in full-time opportunities. Here are some tips that leaders can use to develop and motivate part-time employees!

Offer above average financial compensation. Give your part-time workers a reason to appreciate and be enthusiastic about the work they do. Offer bonuses based on company established incentives. By doing this, you will attract and retain the best part-time workers available and prevent competitors from raiding those who offer the most potential to grow into full-time positions.

Provide a great orientation program. Start off by treating these employees with respect and value. The first impression they are given is important and will make them more productive. Let them know about their assignments, who is allowed to give them work and the basic rules of the workplace. Take the time to review their duties in detail, and let them know what is expected, and what are considered good work skills.

Offer variety in their workload. It is demoralizing to give part-time employees only "grunt work" or mundane boring tasks! Take the time to find out what special skills or talents a part-time worker has. Then give them some tasks that will develop or nurture these skills. Interesting work makes for a better and more fulfilled worker, and it also increases their longevity.

Provide each worker a mentor. Even with good orientation a new worker will become confused and have questions. The best way to make these new workers more effective and make them feel like a part of the team is to assign them a mentor. The mentor should be a full-time worker who has the time and temperament to work with newbies and patiently answer questions.

Offer flextime as a benefit to part-time workers. Allow these workers to have flexible hours to meet their individual needs. Many of these workers have situations that require them to work only part-time. For example, they might be raising children, caring for parents or also working another job. You will retain the better workers by making this perk a distinct advantage in your organization, while reducing costs for the constant retraining of replacement workers. Establish a weekly schedule that accommodates both their needs and the organization's ongoing needs.

Reduce competition and resentment toward part-time workers. From the perspective of full-time workers, the "part-timers" may be considered a threat to their jobs. Make plain to full-time employees that the goal of having a part-time workforce is two-fold. First, they reduce some of the workload of the full-time staff and their employment makes everyone's jobs easier. Secondly, some part-time workers will develop skills that can be incorporated into the organization in the future as new job openings are created.

Think about creative ways you can grow part-time workers into productive and valued staff. The benefit of moving part-timers into the full-time staff is you already know their work habits and skills. On the other hand, they also know your organization well and will blend into the workplace culture more quickly.

Consider that it was Henry I. Kaiser who said, "When your work speaks for itself, don't interrupt."

Chapter 5

A FEW MODERN LEADERSHIP THEORIES

There are literally dozens of leadership theories that have been developed to explain what leadership is all about. Many of these theories are complex and difficult to apply in the real world. I believe communication should be clear and practical. Here are a few modern theories for you to ponder.

THE LEVEL 5 LEADERSHIP STYLE

One of the most frequently asked questions regarding the study of leadership behavior is, "What can make a good company a great company?" Researchers and authors Jim Collins and Jerry Porras believe they have found some important links. They examined this issue in their book entitled *Built to Last: Successful Habits of Visionary Companies*, published by Harper Business, 2002. The authors analyzed eleven companies that started out as good or "competent" organizations, but ended up as "great" by the mid-90's. The definition of great included those who had an outstanding increase in market values at least *eight times* faster than the stock market.

Collins and Porras found that the CEO's of these good to great companies exhibited similar qualities that Collins labeled as *The Level 5 Leadership Style*. According to Collins, Level 5 Leadership is a unique mixture of behaviors, including personal humility and professional will. This style is like a coin with two sides. On one side, Level 5 leaders are calm, modest and accept blame or responsibility when things go wrong. On the other side, they demonstrate a determined resolve to do whatever it takes to produce effective long-term results. They set the highest standards for themselves and others, and accept nothing less. The main behaviors of Level 5 leaders are listed below. Its source is an article by Jim Collins, "Level 5 Leadership," Harvard Business Review, January 2001, p. 73.

I recommend another book by Jim Collins entitled *Good to Great: Why Some Companies Make the Leap... and Others Don't*, published by Harper Collins, 2001.

As you read these qualities, ask yourself how well you measure up? Do these traits describe you? Is there room for improvement in your behavior?

Personal Humility	*Professional Will*
Demonstrates a compelling modesty, shunning public adulation, never boastful.	Creates superb results, a clear catalyst in the transition from good to great.
Acts with quiet, calm determination; relies principally on inspired standards, not inspiring charisma, to motivate others.	Demonstrates an unwavering resolve to do whatever must be done to produce the best long-term results, no matter how difficult.
Channels ambition into the company not the self, sets up successors for even more greatness in the next generation.	Set the standard of building an enduring great company; will settle for nothing less.
Looks in the mirror, not out the window, to apportion responsibility for poor results, never blaming other people, external factors, or bad luck.	Looks out the window, not in the mirror, to apportion credit for the success of the company – to other people, external factors, and good luck.

I encourage you to meditate for one solid week on these qualities and see how your behavior compares to the 5 Level Leadership Style! What can you do to emulate this behavior?

Consider that it was Thomas Edison who wrote, "Three great essentials to achieve anything worthwhile are, first, hard work; second, stick-to-itiveness; third, common sense."

WHAT IS "TRANSFORMATIONAL LEADERSHIP"?

In most areas of the world electrical energy is provided by a power transformer. This boxy device is designed for a simple purpose. It takes the existing energy coming into it and transforms it to a *different* level. Electrical power is transported on a grid system at one voltage and when it arrives at residential neighborhoods it is transformed into a different and useful voltage. Within organizations, the right leadership behaviors can also *transform* the company and individuals from one level to another and produce positive significant change!

In the 1970's, researcher James McGregor Burns wrote a significant book entitled *Leadership*. He sought to define the processes or behaviors used by leaders to motivate or influence followers. Burns described leadership behavior as falling within two broad categories of influence. One category is called *transformational leadership*. This leadership style is founded on the belief that leaders and followers can raise each other to higher levels of motivation and morality. The other category is called *transactional leadership* and is discussed in the next tip.

The heart of transformational leadership is the leader's desire and ability to raise the consciousness of others by appealing to powerful moral values and ideals. The leader is able to transform followers beyond the dishonorable emotions of jealously, greed and fear to higher principles of liberty, justice and humanitarianism. As Burns would say, the followers are raised from their "everyday selves" to become "better selves." Transformational leaders influence followers by serving as teachers, mentors and coaches. They seek to elevate and empower others to a higher level. Transformational leaders can be found within any organization and at any level in the organization. This is a leader that can influence superiors, peers or subordinates.

Bernard Bass expanded upon the earlier ideas of Burns with his own theory of transformational leadership. He defines this supervision in terms of the leader's motivational effect on followers. They feel loyalty, trust, admiration and respect toward the transformational leader. The followers are motivated to serve and achieve more than they originally were expected to. They are inspired to achieve higher-order needs and are made more aware of the organization's needs for their unique skills and talents. Today it is acknowledged that there are four various types of transformational leadership behavior. These are as follows:

1. *Idealized Influence*—This is a behavior that arouses followers to feel a powerful identification and strong emotions toward the leader.

2. *Inspirational Motivation*—A leadership behavior that models high values as an example and includes communication of an inspiring vision. It also promotes powerful symbols to arouse greater effort and a feeling of belonging.

3. *Individualized Consideration*—This behavior provides coaching, support and encouragement of specific followers.

4. *Intellectual Stimulation*—A behavior that influences followers to view problems from a fresh perspective and with a new increased awareness.

The end result of transformational leadership is empowering others to take more initiative in their work, inspiring them to be more committed and building their self-confidence. Of course, these activities can't take place in a vacuum. Transformational leaders *nurture* an organizational culture by giving attention to priorities and concerns. They react maturely to crisis situations, model right behavior, wisely allocate rewards, and define solid measurements for success.

Consider that it was Steven Covey who once wrote, "The goal of transformational leadership is to "transform" people and organizations in a literal sense—to change them in mind and heart; enlarge vision, insight, and understanding; clarify purposes; make behavior congruent with beliefs, principles, or values; and bring about changes that are permanent, self-perpetuating, and momentum building."

WHAT IS "TRANSACTIONAL LEADERSHIP"?

If you study the subject of leadership or read a college textbook on the topic, you will perhaps come across the phrase *transactional leadership* theory. What is this type of leadership behavior, and how does it apply to you? In the 1970's, researcher James McGregor Burns wrote a significant book entitled *Leadership*. He sought to define the processes or behaviors used by leaders to motivate or influence followers. Burns described leadership behavior as falling within two broad categories of influence. One category is called transformational leadership. This leadership style is founded on the belief that leaders and followers can raise each other to higher levels of motivation and morality. *Transformational leadership* was discussed as the previous tip in this book.

In contrast, transactional leadership seeks to motivate followers by appealing to their own self-interest. Its principles are to motivate by the exchange process. For example, business owners exchange status and wages for the work effort of the employee. In the political environment, politicians may exchange favors or government jobs for votes. *Transactional* behavior focuses on the accomplishment of tasks and good worker relationships in exchange for desirable rewards. Transactional leadership may encourage the leader to adapt his or her style and behavior to meet the perceived *expectations* of the followers. Some researchers added to Burns original theory, and it is thought by many today that transactional leadership encompasses *four* types of behavior.

1. *Contingent Reward*—To influence behavior, the leader clarifies the work needed to be accomplished. The leader uses rewards or incentives to achieve results when expectations are met.

2. *Passive Management by Exception*—To influence behavior, the leader uses correction or punishment as a response to unacceptable performance or deviation from the accepted standards.

3. *Active Management by Exception*—To influence behavior,

the leader actively monitors the work performed and uses corrective methods to ensure the work is completed to meet accepted standards.

4. *Laissez-Faire Leadership*—The leader is indifferent and has a "hands-off" approach toward the workers and their performance. This leader ignores the needs of others, does not respond to problems or does not monitor performance.

Transactional leadership behavior is used to one degree or another by most leaders. However, as the old saying goes, "if the only tool in your workbox is a hammer...you will perceive every problem as a nail." A leader should not exclusively or primarily practice transactional leadership behavior to influence others! Here are a few common problems of those who do so. Some use transactional leadership behavior as a tool to manipulate others for selfish personal gain. It can place too much emphasis on the *bottom line*, and by its very nature is short-term oriented with the goal of simply maximizing efficiency and profits. The leader can pressure others to engage in unethical or amoral practices by offering strong rewards or punishments. Transactional leadership seeks to influence others by exchanging work for wages, but it does not build on the workers' need for meaningful work or tap into their creativity. If utilized as the primary behavior by a leader, it can lead to an environment permeated by position, power, perks and politics. The most effective and beneficial leadership behavior to achieve long-term success and improved performance is transformational leadership.

Consider that it was Peter Drucker who once said, "So much of what we call management consists in making it difficult for people to work."

Introduction to Greg L. Thomas

Greg L. Thomas has over 25 years of sales and marketing experience within the electrical manufacturing industry. Some of his positions have included being a National Sales Manager, National Marketing Manager and Regional Sales Manager.

He also has an extensive 35 years experience in public speaking. Greg has provided leadership seminars and keynote speeches for organizations as diverse as Ramapo College, FirstMerit Bank, American Society for Quality, Central Ohio Patient Accounting Managers and the Pennsylvania Governor's Institute. He has also conducted public seminars sponsored by *weLEAD Incorporated*.

Greg has a Master of Arts degree in Leadership from Bellevue University, where he also has served as an adjunct professor teaching courses in business management and leadership. He is the founder and president of *weLEAD Incorporated* and has written articles on the topic of leadership for various publications. Greg and his wife BJ are natives of Cleveland and presently reside in Litchfield, Ohio. His personal web site is located at www.greglthomas.info

weLEAD Incorporated

weLEAD Incorporated is a major online resource for leadership development. Founded as a nonprofit organization in 2001, it provides hundreds of free articles, book reviews and valuable tips to promote positive leadership values. *weLEAD* also publishes a monthly online magazine that specializes in personal leadership development and in teaching servant leadership principles to organizations.

Greg L. Thomas and other *weLEAD* associates are available to provide keynotes addresses or workshops for virtually any organization or convention. Feel free to contact Greg at gthomas@leadingtoday.org

We also encourage you to visit our site located at www.leadingtoday.org

This and other quality books are available from

OverLookedBooks

Visit us online at:
www.overlookedbooks.com

LaVergne, TN USA
29 November 2009
165425LV00003B/167/A